Great Clothing from Sweatshirts, T-Shirts & Denim

Susan P. Beck

Great Clothing from
Sweatshirts, T-Shirts & Denim

Susan P. Beck

A Sterling/Sewing Information Resources Book

Sewing Information Resources

Owner: JoAnn Pugh-Gannon
Photography: Kaz Ayukawa, K Graphics
Book Design and Page Layout: Rose Sheifer, Graphic Productions
Illustrations: Pauline Phung
Copy Editor: Barbara Patterson
Index: Anne Leach

Library of Congress Cataloging-in-Publication Data available

A Sterling/Sewing Information Resources Book

2 4 6 8 10 9 7 5 3 1

Published by Sterling Publishing Company, Inc.
387 Park Avenue South, New York, N.Y. 10016
Produced by Sewing Information Resources
P.O. Box 330, Wasco, Il. 60183
©1998 by Susan Beck
Distributed in Canada by Sterling Publishing
c/o Canadian Manda Group, One Atlantic Avenue, Suite 105
Toronto, Ontario, Canada, N6K 3E7
Distributed in Great Britain and Europe by Cassell PLC
Wellington House, 125 Strand, London WC2R 0BB, England
Distributed in Australia by Capricorn Link (Australia) Pty Ltd.
P.O. Box 6651, Baulkham Hills, Business Centre, NSW 2153, Australia
Printed in the United States of America
All rights reserved.

Sterling ISBN 0-8069-0792-4

Table of Contents

Acknowledgments

First of all, this book could not have been written without the confidence that JoAnn Pugh-Gannon placed in me when she asked me to write it. Her support and encouragement helped to pull it all together in a relatively short time. It is a pleasure to work with someone that has such a high standard of quality and a dedication to excellence.

A major source of inspiration for many of the projects in this book came from a relatively new, but already very close friend, Anna Marie Connally. Not only did she help keep me on track, but she contributed several of the projects. The "Bed" Jacket, the Denim Overvest, the Two-Piece Shirt and Skirt, the Dressed-up Sandals, and the Zippered Tote, all came from her creative mind. It's fun to have a friend who shares the same loves—God, family, and sewing. I know this will be the first of many collaborative projects we do together.

Introduction

I never could follow a pattern. It isn't that I can't read, and the patterns I selected were not all that difficult. There was just something about going from point A to point B to point C until I had worked my way through the alphabet that didn't appeal to me. I would start in the middle, move back to the beginning, and eventually get to the end, sometimes quicker and easier than the pattern directed, sometimes slower and harder, but always with a sense of satisfaction that I had done it my way.

One of my favorite books as a young girl was *Gone With the Wind*, and I enjoyed the movie even more. There were lots of reasons why I liked it so, but one was the resourcefulness of the heroine, Scarlett O'Hara. Always looking for a way to come out on top, she made use of whatever she could find in those war-torn days. I loved the way she transformed the drab and tattered green velvet draperies into a beautiful gown, making ingenious use of the only fabric available to her.

Unlike Scarlett, we have access to all types of fabrics at more than affordable prices, but there is still a charm to creatively using what you have to make something quite wonderful. Creativity takes over when we see a beautiful tablecloth and it becomes a skirt. Or a faded sheet becomes a hand-dyed embroidered blouse. Looking at materials around us in a new light and imagining what they can be inspires us to look beyond the pattern, beyond traditional fabrics, to see what we can create.

This book offers only a few of the hundreds of ways that this can be done. But hopefully it will start your creative juices flowing and give you the spirit to explore the possibilities of creative clothing.

Chapter One

The Creative Process

Creativity seems to defy definition. Most people believe creativity is inborn. Not so. Creativity can be cultivated, especially in the world of sewing and crafts. But you have to be willing to play the game and enjoy the process or your budding creativity will be stifled and suppressed. You must be able to throw out the rules, think upside down, and look at things with new eyes.

> Creativity is a type of learning process where the teacher and pupil are located in the same individual.
> —Arthur Koestler

Creativity and imagination go hand in hand. If you are conditioned to be unimaginative and reserved, you may need to rethink some old habits. The American school system that most of us were a part of for 12+ years is based on concrete facts and figures with a finite beginning and end. We memorized, calculated, and colored within the lines. We learned early on that there was one right answer and many wrong ones for every problem. We played by the rules to get the grades, followed directions to gain acceptance, and repeated by rote to excel in a subject.

There is nothing wrong with this type of learning, and, for subjects such as mathematics, there is a definite right answer to most problems. However, when learning and problem solving are approached in this way over the course of our most formative years, it is not surprising that many of us feel our creatively is stifled. Creativity flourishes in an atmosphere of freedom. Freedom to think and do, freedom to try and fail, and freedom to be accepted no matter what harebrained idea you come up with.

If these freedoms bother you, you are probably not fully experiencing your creativity. There are specific steps you can take to foster your imagination. Once you understand the creative process, and focus more on being inventive and ingenious, you will find it becomes second nature. Inventiveness and originality seem to feed each other, growing over time to influence your way of thinking.

The Process

There are basically five steps to the creative process. Each one is distinct but not necessarily separate from the others. Being creative is not an orderly process. It does not move from Point A to Point B to Point C. If you drew a diagram of creativity, it would not resemble a neat chart where every step has a place. It would more likely resemble a spider web made by a not-too-accomplished spider, with many steps overlapping and running into each other.

The first step in the process is *gathering*. Information, ideas, inspiration—these are the things you must constantly be on the lookout for. Everywhere you turn there are hundreds of impressions that can be turned into designs and useful creations. Learn to open your eyes and see the quilting design in the wallpaper, the embellishment technique in the flower garden, and the neckline style in the architecture of a building. Carry a small notepad at all times, or a few 3" x 5" cards, for jotting down inspirations and ideas. Even if you can't use that terrific design idea now, file it away. It may be the perfect thing on down the road. Many of the ideas in this book are ones that I had put in a file over the years, because I knew I would have a use for them...someday.

> I invent nothing.
> I rediscover.
> —Auguste Rodin

The second step is *visualizing*. This could be described as a brainstorming session with yourself. Let any idea take shape no matter how unusual or outlandish it may seem. Don't censor your thoughts and don't prejudge any pathway before exploring it. Follow these thoughts through to their conclusion before determining whether they will work or not. Even if an idea doesn't work, it will likely spark another one or two that will. Again, writing these thoughts down will help to crystallize and define them. It may also be helpful to carry a small voice recorder to collect the best of these brainstorming sessions.

> The more you reason, the less you create.
> —Raymond Chandler

Formulating is the third step. Take all the data you have input into your computer of a brain, including all of your notes and recordings, and turn them into a plan. This is sometimes accomplished by sitting down and mapping out a strategy with a definite beginning and a definite ending. Or it may be done intuitively, almost subconsciously, as the ideas germinate into a full-blown vision of what to do. This often happens to me at one of two times—when I am falling asleep or when I am waking up.

Somewhere in that dreamy land between sleeping and wakefulness, my brain is able to sort out all the data I have put into it and come to a workable conclusion. And, of course, I have a pencil and paper near to record these sudden bursts of originality. On the occasions

when I just can't fully wake to make a few notes, I convince myself that I will remember my inspiration until I arise on my schedule. And I do. I remember that I had a fabulous idea that would make me happier, richer, or more beautiful, but I rarely remember the idea itself. So get in the habit of writing it down.

Another time when the subconscious takes over is when you are actually asleep. Ideas and solutions will sometimes be worked out in dreams. Elias Howe, the inventor of the sewing machine, was trying to perfect his invention, but was having trouble with a key component, the needle. He just couldn't seem to get it right. After struggling with it for years, he had a dream. He was being chased by cannibals with spears. He was given 24 hours to complete the machine or the cannibals would kill him. As the cannibals approached, he was able to take a close look at their spears and he noticed that all of the spears had small holes in the tips—thus the design for the sewing machine needle. Again, the trick is to remember what you dream. It is best to write or record the dream as soon as you wake. Otherwise, even if you remember the premise of the dream, the details may be lost, and it is often the details that are the most important.

> I waited for the idea to consolidate, for the grouping and composition of themes to settle themselves in my brain. When I felt I held enough cards, I determined to pass to action and did so.
>
> —Claude Monet

Perfecting is the next step in the process. Taking the idea and evaluating and refining it to see what works and what doesn't. This is where the really hard work begins; where the acceptance of failure is important. Few designing or creating at-

> *In creating, the only hard thing's to begin; a grass blade's no easier to make than an oak.*
>
> — James Russell Lowell.

tempts are successful on the first try. But much can be learned from each failure, even if it is simply what *not* to do next time. Thomas Edison tried over 1,000 filaments before he finally came up with a lightbulb that actually worked. So don't get discouraged when things do *not* go smoothly—just keep looking at the ways an idea *won't* work and eventually you'll come up with at least one way that it will.

Perseverance is the step that follows the first four and is probably the most difficult. This is often where other people get involved. Whether you are trying to market a new invention or wearing your latest design, at some time you will have to deal with critics. Fortunately, not everyone has the same likes, dislikes, and sense of mediocrity. It would certainly be a dull world if the opposite were true. However, this means that somewhere, someone is not going to agree with your idea. You must be prepared for this and make a decision to remember how excited you were when it first came to you. How it delighted and enthralled you as you looked at it from all angles, refining it and making it completely your own. And even though there may be dissenters and naysayers in the crowd, you should begin developing patience and courage as you strive toward success.

> I don't know the key to success, but the key to failure is trying to please everybody.
>
> —Bill Cosby

Now that you have an idea of the mechanics of creativity, let's look at some exercises that will help you make a conscious shift to creative thinking. If you deliberately choose to shake up your normal patterns of perception, it will become easier and more natural to think creatively. One exercise that you can do is visual brainstorming: the practice of thinking freely in pictures without words. It may sound more difficult than it is. Most people at one time or another have picked up a pencil and doodled aimlessly on paper, drawing pictures and cartoons as they popped into their heads without any thought of what they were drawing or why. This is usually done out of boredom. Try doodling on purpose. Choose a particular problem that you are trying to solve. For instance, you have one of those lovely bridesmaid's dresses in your closet and you hate to get rid of it, but you know you will never wear it again. There must be something for which it could be used. But what? Knowing what design or purpose you want gives you a plan of action. However, if you are not sure where to begin, here's another exercise that may help you get moving. It's often difficult to know what you want, but most of us have little trouble knowing what we don't want. Try a little opposite thinking when you are stuck for ideas. When you are trying to figure out what to make from that beautiful green silk that has been in your stash for five years, think about what you *don't* want. You don't want a winter coat from it, you don't want a casual pullover, and you don't want a three piece suit. Continue through the list and you may be surprised that you soon arrive at what you *do* want.

Start doodling and see what appears. Move from one idea to another without any real motive or design. Use a large piece of paper and don't worry about your drawing skills. You know what you're drawing and that's all that's important. After a while take an objective look at the results; you may be surprised at what you see. This exercise helps you make your thoughts tangible and concrete. You can see the progression of ideas, one leading to another, possibly ending in a solution.

Another similar exercise is to pick up a pen and start writing. This time put words instead of pictures on the paper. It may be difficult to begin, but once started it's amazing what your train of thought can produce. This is similar to keeping a journal, however, instead of making short entries day by day, select a certain time frame or a particular number of pages to write. Just begin and write for, say, 20 minutes or until you have filled three pages. Look back over your thoughts when you are finished, but also look them over again several days later when you can be more objective.

When trying to come up with a creative solution, it is sometimes difficult to know where to begin The best thing to do is to take action, but exactly *what* action is the question. Following is a list of words related to sewing techniques and designing. If you don't know where to start, review the list and apply each one to the situation at hand. If you are trying to design a new dress for that high school reunion, but have no idea what you want, picture each of these elements, turn it over in your mind, and try to visualize the dress with it. Add any of your own favorites that are missing and keep this handy when you need some direction in your design thinking.

๏ pleating	๏ passementerie	๏ bias binding
๏ couching	๏ ribbon weaving	๏ bias-cut fabrics
๏ cutwork	๏ pintucks	๏ color blocking
๏ satin stitch appliqué	๏ heirloom sewing	๏ hand-dyed fabrics
๏ shadow work	๏ single needle tucks	๏ welt pockets
๏ patchwork	๏ texturized fabrics	๏ raglan sleeves
๏ quilting	๏ charted needlework	๏ double breasted
๏ bobbin work	๏ blind appliqué	๏ drop shouldered
๏ battenberg	๏ stained glass appliqué	๏ princess seamed
๏ embroidery	๏ silk ribbon embroidery	๏ ruffles

Designing and redesigning clothing began with Adam and Eve and the figleaf. It has certainly progressed since then with many elements entering into it. For those of us who enjoy this process, there are basically three reasons we do it. We design because of need. We need a solution to a problem, such as making a good impression at a job interview. This type of clothing construction often has a built-in solution. Once we decide what it will take to make a good physical impression, we see the path to take and the clothing to make.

> If I see an ending, I can work backwards.
> —Arthur Miller

> Our vision begins with our desires.
> — Audre Lorde

A second reason to sew and design clothing is because of style; we want to make a personal statement. Most designers have a firm idea of their own style and statement. It is often unusual and different from the style of the masses. There is an inner need to express and show this originality. It drives the designer to create and construct with self expression as the goal.

Self-satisfaction is a third factor in the design process. It's fun and personally satisfying to know that a garment or accessory is of your own design or making. The knowledge that you have used your creativity and invented or reinvented a design gives you fulfillment and gratification that other pursuits do not.

> When I can no longer create, I'll be done for.
> —Coco Chanel

Chapter Two

Designing Creative Clothing

Materials and Supplies

When creating or re-creating a piece of clothing, there are very few limits to the materials and supplies that can be used. Any item of fabric, new or used, becomes a potential source of material. Any non-fabric item is a possible closure, accessory, or embellishment material. Be on the lookout, no matter where you are, for potential sources of materials and supplies.

Purchased materials, such as fabric yardage, laces, silk flowers, trims, and buttons are the traditional materials most seamstresses use when approaching a new project. But don't stop there. Look at existing items such as linens, blankets, and ready-made articles of clothing and picture the possibilities. A mediocre garment can be changed into something spectacular with a little imagination and a few scraps of fabric and trims.

Leftover materials such as remnants, scraps, odd buttons, beads, and trims offer opportunities for creative expression. The challenge to create an exciting design becomes stronger when the amount or type of material available is limited to what you have on hand. The designs are often more interesting and unusual when you work within the confines of chosen materials.

Found materials such as shells, rocks, driftwood, or old jewelry can offer unusual applications for embellishments or garment closures. The key is to never let conventional boundaries determine the usefulness of any fabric or material when creating your own unique look. Keep your mind open to any and all possibilities when determining the value of materials.

Color, Balance, Harmony

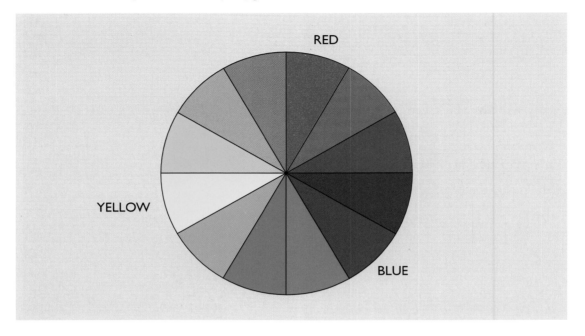

When creating an article of clothing or a unique accessory, the basic elements of good design apply. The overall look and feel of the design should be considered and evaluated with color, balance, and harmony in mind.

In deciding upon a color scheme, the choice is really a personal one. Even though there are some guidelines to consider, the bottom line is that you should enjoy the chosen colors and respond to the way they interact with each other. Consulting a color wheel will give you an idea of the way the colors are related and how they can affect each other. For instance, complementary colors, those opposite each other on the wheel, have a very strong reaction to each other and offer vivid and intense results when placed side by side. Analogous colors appear next to each other on the color wheel and are good to use when blending colors or graduating from one to another.

As a general rule, warm colors such as red, yellow, and orange seem to advance or move toward the eye. Cool colors such as blue, purple, and green recede, or move away from it. The choice of colors can set the tone for the garment by evoking certain emotional responses. The responses are often personal as people have different feelings about the same colors; however, warm colors often evoke feelings of passion or aggression while cool colors are more likely to cause feelings of restfulness and calmness.

If selecting a color scheme is difficult for you, a simple way to make a choice is to go fabric shopping. Without regard for the type, weight, or potential use of the fabric, survey the bolts until you find a multicolored print that suits the emotions of the project you have in mind. Inspect the print and isolate two to five colors that will work as a grouping for the project. Choose one dominant color with one or two others as accents in fairly large amounts. Add one or two additional colors in small amounts for added interest. The colors used in lesser amounts are often the strongest colors and can give depth to the overall feel of the color scheme.

The important thing is not to be afraid of color. You know what colors you like, and what you like is appropriate for the design you are creating. So make your selections based on your intuition and in the end you will enjoy the coloration of your design.

The design should be balanced, which does not mean that everything should be uniform and even. The style can be symmetrical (equal) or asymmetrical (uneven). Either type of design can be balanced through the use of color, embellishments, and/or visual weight. There should be a feeling of evenness in the design, so that one area does not overpower the rest of the project. As you develop the design, step away from it and evaluate the overall look of the design rather than focusing on one portion.

The project should have a feeling of harmony that blends the colors, fabric prints, embellishments, lines, and textures. These elements should be related in some way so that they do not fight each other and cause discord within the design. For instance, bold, geometric shapes do not usually blend well with dainty, curling, floral motifs.

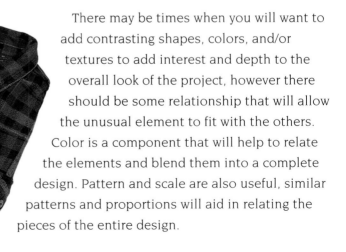

There may be times when you will want to add contrasting shapes, colors, and/or textures to add interest and depth to the overall look of the project, however there should be some relationship that will allow the unusual element to fit with the others. Color is a component that will help to relate the elements and blend them into a complete design. Pattern and scale are also useful, similar patterns and proportions will aid in relating the pieces of the entire design.

Fashion Blanks

When beginning a design, it is sometimes difficult to know where to start. Usually there is something that sparks the desire to create. This may be something concrete, such as wanting a new jacket to wear with jeans, or it may be more abstract, such as falling in love with a particular fabric. A good way to get started is to doodle as in the creativity exercise discussed in the first chapter. This time, however, focus the doodling on a specific canvas. Use fashion blanks to concentrate the ideas into a garment design. Fashion blanks are simply line drawings of garments that can serve as blank canvases on which to design. Collect photographs and drawings of various styles of garments from magazines, pattern books, and catalogs. Using a black marker and white paper, trace the outline of the garments (fashion blanks) shown at the beginning of each chapter and use them for developing designs. Once traced, the garments can be photocopied and used over and over again. You will want to develop several designs before making a final choice, and you may want to use the same basic garment style with a different creative twist for a future project. Fashion blanks are included throughout this book showing several styles of various types of garments. Trace and photocopy these to begin your creative clothing collection.

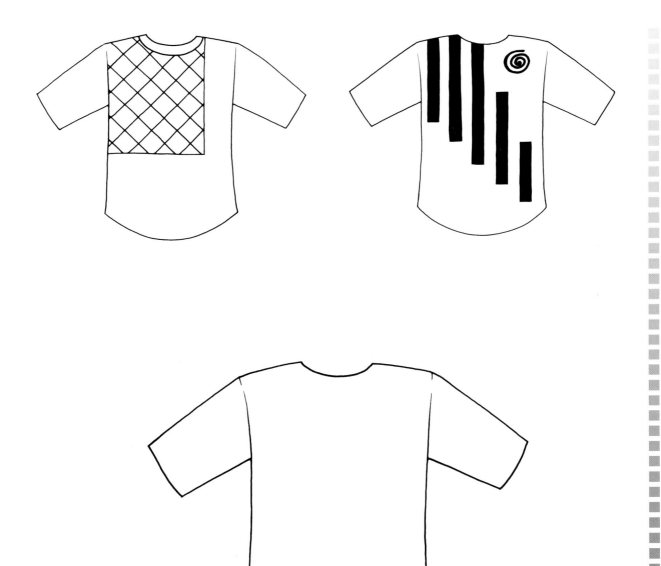

Start here by tracing this shirt. Begin doodling before working on your actual garment.

Chapter Three

Terrific Tops

Blouses, shirts, and tops all have one thing in common—they are all made to wear with another article of clothing such as a skirt, a pair of slacks, or shorts. Beyond that they can be widely diverse, ranging from comfy and casual to sleek and elegant. Almost any type of fabric can be used to make a top and the details and embellishments can be anything from patchwork to beads.

The tops shown in this chapter all begin with a ready-made garment. They are then modified by adding fabrics and trims, ribbon stitching, beading, patchwork, and other techniques to create unique looks for updating your wardrobe.

Country Camp Shirt

Make a cute country top embellished with patchwork hems and turned up sleeves from a man's casual shirt.

- Man's casual, short sleeved shirt
- Fat quarters (22" x 18") of five coordinating fabrics
- Decorative button for pocket
- Fabric marker
- Seam ripper
- Shoulder pads (optional)

1. Select a shirt that is slightly large for a loose, comfortable feel. Create a new lower edge, cutting it off about 3" below the waistline or where desired. Using a seam ripper, remove the pocket.

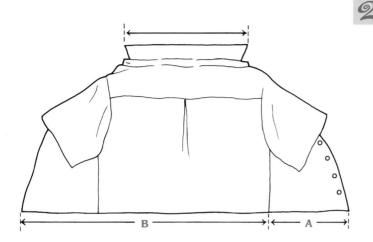

2. Trace around the removed pocket, adding ¼" seam allowances along all edges. For measurement A, measure from the side seam to the center front on the right side of the shirt. Add ½" to this measurement for seam allowances. For measurement B, measure from the right side seam, around the back, to the center front of the left side of the shirt. Add ½" to this measurement for seam allowances. Measure the collar from one front edge to the other and add 1".

3. To create the checkerboard hem, cut two contrasting fabric strips, 2" each x the width of the fabric. Using a ¼" seam allowance, seam the two strips along one long side. Press the seam allowance to the darker fabric.

4. Cut the joined strips into 2" segments. Stitch the segments together, turning every other one to create a checkerboard effect. You will need a checkerboard strip to equal measurement A and one to equal measurement B.

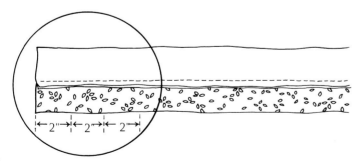

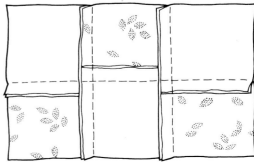

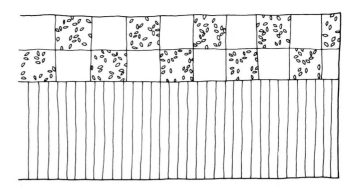

5 Cut a piece of fabric as wide as measurement A and 4½" long. Stitch checkerboard A to this fabric across the width.

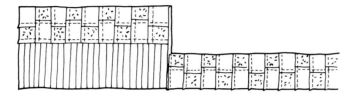

6 Place checkerboard B, right sides together, with the side of the checkerboard A unit. Stitch the fabric and the checkerboard together.

7 Starting at the right side seam of the shirt and continuing around the remaining lower edge, place the lower edge of the right side of the checkerboard to the *wrong* side of the shirt and pin. Stitch, using a ¼" seam allowance.

8 Fold the checkerboard to the right side and press, turning under ¼" at the front opening of the shirt. Baste the upper edge of the checkerboard to the shirt.

9 Cut three 2" x 22" strips of fabric. Stitch two of them together to make one strip to equal measurement B. Trim the other strip to equal measurement A.

10 Fold the strips in half lengthwise and press. Place them along the basted upper edge of the checkerboards with the raw edges even. Stitch in place. Fold up over the raw edges and edgestitch.

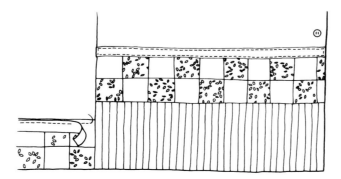

11 To create the collar, cut a strip 2" by the collar measurement from step 2. Fold the raw edges in to the center, wrong sides together, and press. Position the strip along the center of the collar, folding the ends under the front edge of the collar. Stitch in place along each side of the strip.

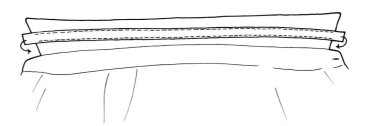

 12 Cut one pocket and one lining from the pattern.

 13 Cut one 3" square. Fold the square in half across the diagonal. Fold the side points down to the center point to create a prairie point. Cut the prairie point in half across the diagonal. Place the prairie point right side up on the right side of the pocket with the raw edge of the upper prairie point even with the upper raw edge of the pocket. Baste in place.

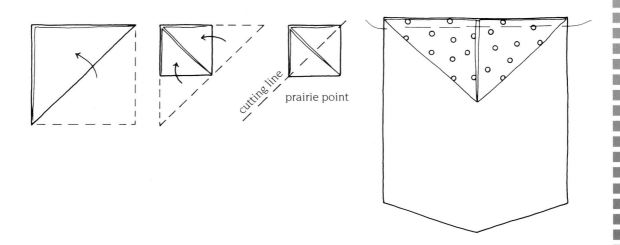

cutting line

prairie point

 14 Place the lining right side down on the pocket and stitch along all sides, leaving an opening for turning. Trim, turn, and press.

15 Stitch a button on the prairie point through all layers.

16 Position the pocket on the shirt where the original pocket was removed. Edgestitch the sides and lower edges to secure the pocket in place.

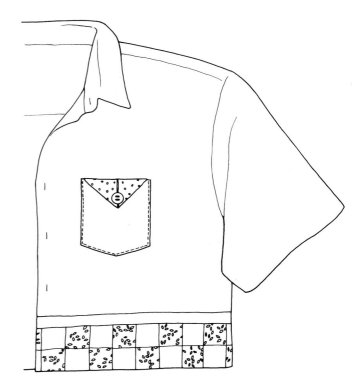

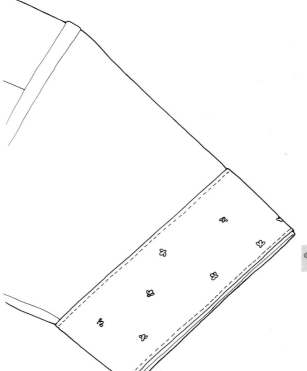

17 Measure the distance around the lower edge of the sleeve. Cut two strips of fabric, $4\frac{1}{2}$" x the width of the sleeve. Fold in half and stitch across the short end to form a tube. Press.

18 Fold $\frac{1}{2}$" to the wrong side on each side of the tube. Press. Turn the shirt wrong side out. Slip one of the tubes over the sleeve and position it at the lower edge of the sleeve. Stitch in place along both edges of the tube.

19 Turn the shirt to the right side and press the sleeves. Fold the sleeves up twice and tack the cuffs at the underarm seam. Add shoulder pads if desired.

Silk Ribbon Sweater

Add stripes of color to a plain sweater with the delicate look of silk ribbon embroidery and beading. The color is randomly placed across the front of the sweater with each stripe ending in a bloom of silk ribbon.

- One loosely knit sweater with a vertical rib or stripe design
- Assorted colors of 4mm silk ribbon
- Large tapestry needle with a blunt point
- Regular hand sewing needle
- Sewing thread in a color to match the sweater
- Small seed beads or pearls
- Beading needle
- Beading thread
- Disappearing fabric marker
- Small ruler

1. Determine where the stripes of color will be placed on the front of the sweater. They can be stitched in each rib or stripe or evenly spaced by skipping a chosen number of stripes. Along each stripe where the ribbon is to be stitched, starting at the lower edge, mark the stripe in 1½" increments using the fabric marker.

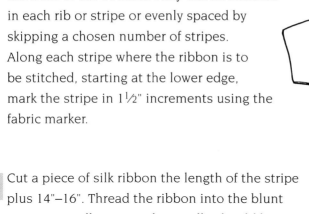

2. Cut a piece of silk ribbon the length of the stripe plus 14"–16". Thread the ribbon into the blunt tapestry needle. **Note:** The needle should be quite large in order to make a hole big enough for the ribbon to lie flat. The hole made in the sweater will not show because it will be filled with the ribbon.

3. Starting at the lower edge of the sweater, bring the ribbon up from the wrong side at the first mark, leaving a 2"–3" tail. On the wrong side of the lower edge of the sweater, trim the silk ribbons and fold the edges under. Using thread to match the sweater and a regular hand sewing needle, take several small stitches to secure the ribbon to the sweater.

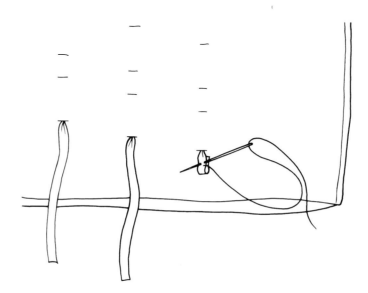

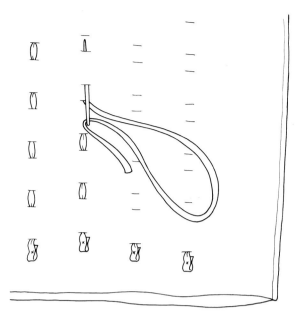

Stitch along the stripe with a running stitch, taking 1" stitches and spacing them ½" apart. Continue stitching to the top of the sweater, making sure the ribbon remains flat.

4 At the end of the stripe, use the lazy daisy stitch to create a flower with five to seven petals. Pull the ribbon to the wrong side and secure by taking a few small stitches through the ribbon only.

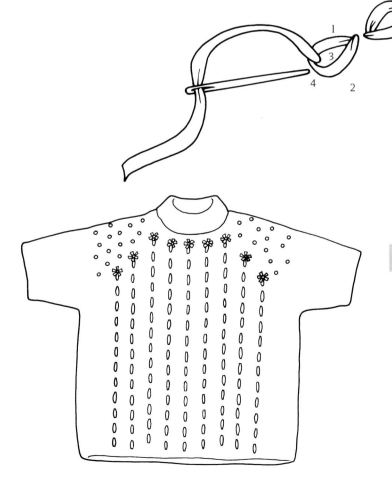

5 Stitch small beads or pearls in the center of each flower using a beading needle and thread.

Optional Design Idea: Scatter beads randomly across the upper portion of the sweater where the flowers are stitched.

Crop-Top Sweatshirt

Take a sweatshirt and turn it into a top
trimmed with piping and a print. Short sleeves
and a cropped length give it a fresh new look.
The print fabric bands are actually reverse
facings that finish the edges as they add color.

- One sweatshirt
- ½ yard of coordinating print fabric
- ¼ yard of solid fabric to accent the print
- 2 yards of ¼" cable cording
- Three ⅜" decorative buttons the same color as the piping
- One package single-fold bias tape to match the shirt

1. Cut the lower band of ribbing off of the sweatshirt. The cut shirt should be about 4" below the waist. Cut the sleeves off at the bend of the elbow. Cut off the neckline ribbing.

2. Measure the distance around the lower edge of the shirt and add ½". Cut a band of the printed fabric using this measurement x 5½".

3. With right sides together, seam the strip with a ¼" seam allowance to make a circle.

4. From the solid, complimentary fabric, cut and piece enough bias strips to go around the upper edge of the band. Wrap the bias strip around the cord and, using a zipper or piping foot, stitch next to the cord. Stitch this piping along the upper edge of the band.

5. Place the right side of the printed band against the wrong side of the shirt matching the lower edges. Using a ¼" seam allowance, stitch the band to the shirt. Turn the printed band to the right side of the shirt and press.

6. Turn under the piping along the top edge of the band and pin to the shirt. Stitch the band to the shirt, stitching in the ditch of the seam between the piping and the printed band. Edgestitch the lower edge of the shirt.

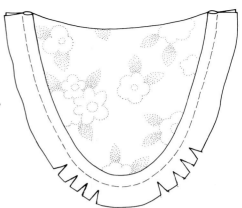

7 Repeat the above steps to finish the lower edges of the sleeves, cutting a 3" band.

8 Using the pattern provided in the back of the book, cut an accent piece for the front neckline. Add piping to all edges, except the upper neck edge. For a smooth curve, clip the seam allowance of the piping as you stitch. Trim the cord from inside of the piping along the neck edges of the accent piece.

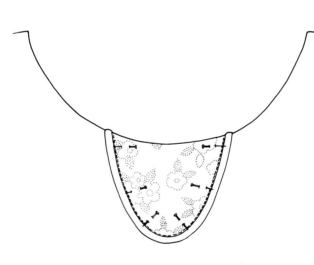

9 Pin the accent piece to the shirt, matching the center fronts. Stitch the piece to the shirt, stitching in the ditch of the seam created by stitching the piping to the accent piece.

10 Face the neck edge with bias tape. After stitching the bias tape to the shirt, turn it to the inside and press Edgestitch the neckline and topstitch $\frac{1}{4}$" away from the edgestitching.

11 Add decorative buttons down the center of the accent piece.

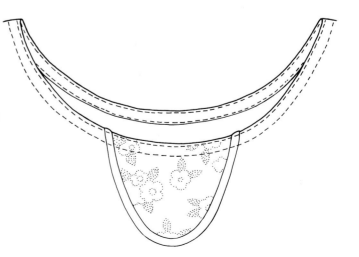

Trimmed Tunic

Turn a man's shirt or a seldom-worn blouse into a terrific tunic using a coordinating fabric and braided trim. Great to wear over leggings, slacks, or stretch pants.

- One shirt-type blouse with a stand-up collar
- ½ yard of fabric that blends well with the blouse
- 3 yards of flat braided trim in a coordinating color
- 10" square of fusible interfacing
- Coordinating buttons—two more than originally on the shirt
- Shoulder pads (optional)

1 To determine the length to add to the blouse, measure the distance from the center of one button to the center of the next. Multiply by 2 and add ½" for seam allowances.

Open the blouse flat and measure the distance from the right front edge to the left front edge; add 6".

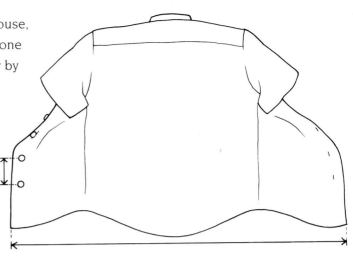

 2 Cut a strip of fabric across the coordinating fabric using the above measurements. Measure one-third up from the bottom and cut the shirt apart.

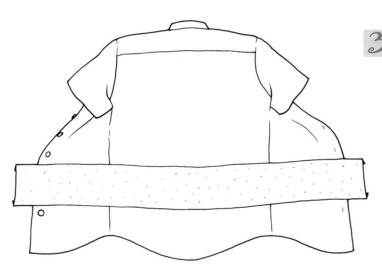

3 Fuse interfacing to 6" at each end of the insert strip on the wrong side of the fabric and finish the two short ends by serging or overcasting. Serge or overcast the strip to the cut edges of the shirt with about 3" extending at each front edge.

Press the seam allowance toward the strip. Fold the ends of the strip into the inside of the shirt and stitch to the shirt.

4 Sew two new buttonholes on the inserted fabric piece, continuing the spacing of the original shirt. Replace the buttons on the shirt, adding two for the new buttonholes.

 5 Carefully remove the pocket(s) from the shirt. Cut a piece of trim 1" wider than the pocket. Stitch about one-third of the distance from the top, folding the excess at each side to the wrong side.

Stitch the decorated pocket(s) in place.

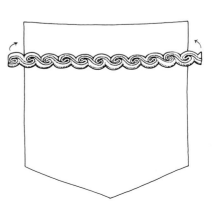

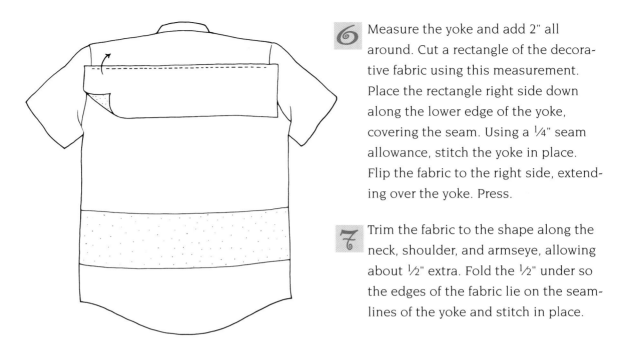

6 Measure the yoke and add 2" all around. Cut a rectangle of the decorative fabric using this measurement. Place the rectangle right side down along the lower edge of the yoke, covering the seam. Using a 1/4" seam allowance, stitch the yoke in place. Flip the fabric to the right side, extending over the yoke. Press.

7 Trim the fabric to the shape along the neck, shoulder, and armseye, allowing about 1/2" extra. Fold the 1/2" under so the edges of the fabric lie on the seamlines of the yoke and stitch in place.

8 Cut the sleeves off at the elbow. Cut a 2" strip of fabric to go around the lower edge of each sleeve. Fold the fabric strip right sides together and stitch to form a circle.

9 Place the right side of the circle against the wrong side of the sleeve with the lower raw edges even. Stitch along the lower edge of the sleeve using a 1/4" seam allowance. Turn the fabric to the right side of the sleeve and press. Pin or baste in place. Stitch trim over the raw edge of the fabric band to finish.

10 Stitch flat trim over the lower seam of the stand-up collar. Add shoulder pads to the shirt if desired.

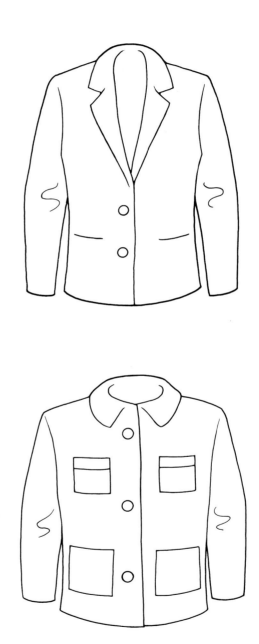

Chapter Four

Creative Coats

A coat or jacket can be worn as protection against the elements or it can become a fashion statement. More than any piece in your wardrobe, the jacket can be a useful tool in creating your own look. Throw a jacket over a plain outfit and upgrade it to a coordinated suit of clothing. Pull together some unrelated pieces by wearing a great jacket over them.

In this chapter, the jackets range from an understated knit cardigan to a casual denim car coat to an elegant Victorian tuxedo. They all offer different looks and will add panache to any outfit.

Victorian Tuxedo

Start with a man's tuxedo jacket and embellish it with crazy patchwork to add glamour and elegance. Wear it over a simple pair of slacks with a lace camisole for an elegant evening outfit. The embellishment is stitched onto a felt "shawl" which is then stitched to the shoulders of the jacket. Trim the pockets and add a distinctive button or button cover to complete the look.

- Man's tuxedo jacket
- ½ yard of black felt
- ½ yard of thin fleece or batting
- Assorted pieces of fabric (velvet, velveteen, tapestry, lame, etc.) in rich colors such as burgundy, black, and gold
- Assorted pieces of trims and laces
- Decorative buttons, trinkets, beads, and charms
- Metallic threads and decorative cords for couching and bobbinwork
- Wide lace or fringe for the outer edge of the shawl
- ½"-wide flat braid or trim for the inner edge of the shawl
- Decorative button(s) or button cover(s) for the jacket front

1 Using the pattern in the back of the book, cut a shawl from black felt and one from fleece. Place the fleece shawl on top of the felt one and pin or baste in place. Check the fit of the shawl to your jacket.

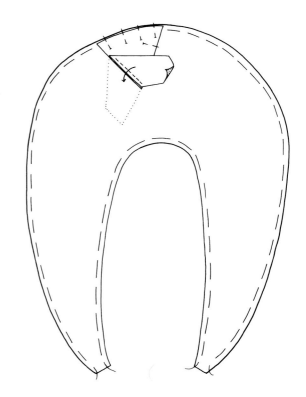

2 Beginning near the center back of the shawl, place a small piece of fabric right side up and pin in place. Position a second piece of fabric right side down and stitch along one edge of the first. Flip the second piece to the right side and press. Trim the fabrics if necessary.

3 Continue adding various pieces of fabrics as desired using the "flip and sew" technique until the entire shawl is covered. Insert laces and trims into some of the seams before stitching or add trims to cover the seams.

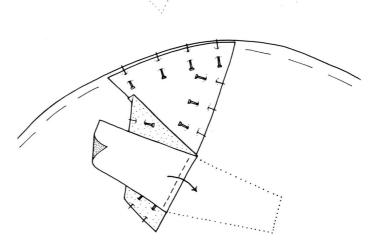

4 Once the entire shawl is covered with the patchwork piecing, add bobbinwork and decorative stitching as desired using rayon and metallic threads. Randomly couch decorative cords or metallic threads over the piecing and add beading as desired. Add additional trims and clusters of buttons.

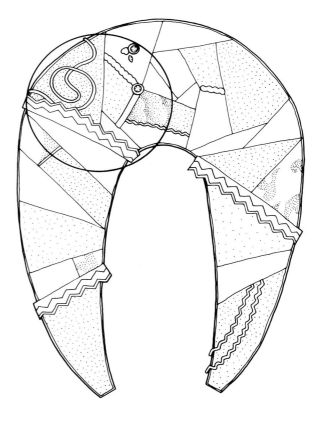

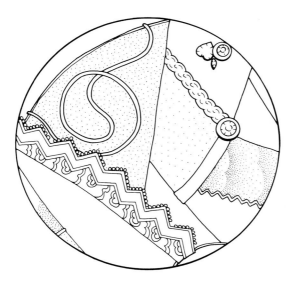

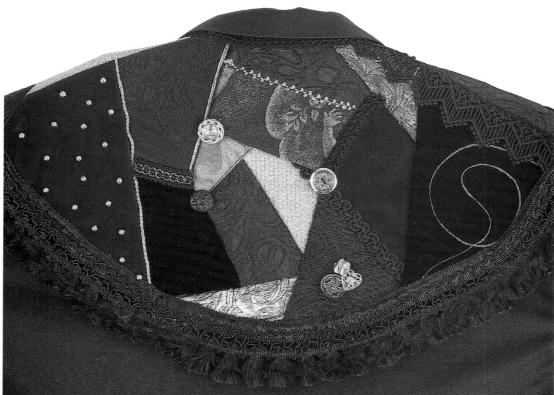

5 Serge the inner and outer edges of the shawl using black serger thread and a 3-thread overlock stitch.

6 Stitch the fringe along the outer edges of the shawl, folding the lower front edges under. Stitch the flat braid over the inner edge of the shawl.

7 Position the shawl over the shoulders of the jacket and pin in place. Hand stitch the inner edge of the shawl to the jacket only, avoiding stitching through the facings and linings. Tack the outer edge of the shawl to the jacket at the shoulders.

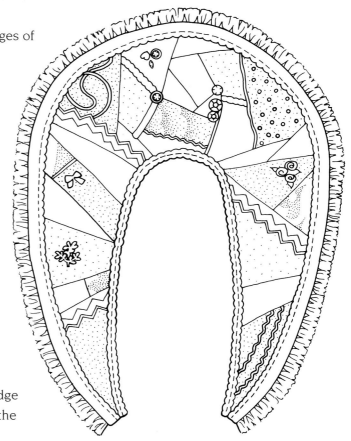

8 Add trim and/or lace to the pocket edges by hand stitching it to the pocket opening.

9 Replace the button(s) of the jacket with decorative button(s) or button cover(s).

Plaid-Trimmed Jacket

This simple jacket starts with a sweatshirt and several small pieces of plaid fabrics.
Start with an extra large sweatshirt to make a truly asymmetrical look.

- Sweatshirt with set-in sleeves (raglan sleeves will not allow for a smooth binding over the seam). Select a sweatshirt at least one size too large if an asymmetrical overlap is desired.
- Four to five pieces (at least 12" square) of different plaid fabrics
- One large decorative button
- Shoulder pads (optional)

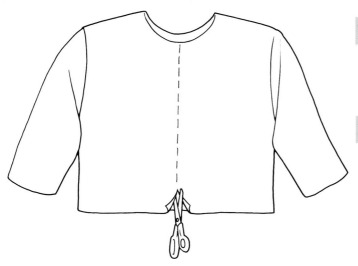

 Carefully cut the neck, sleeve, and lower ribbing from the sweatshirt. The ribbing can be saved for a future project.

2. Determine the center front of the sweatshirt and draw a line from the neck to the lower edge. Cut the front along the drawn line.

3. Turn the sweatshirt wrong side out. Narrow the sleeves by tapering from under the arm to the wrist as desired. Be sure the wrist opening will accommodate the size of your hand. Taper the front neckline from the shoulderline to the center front as desired.

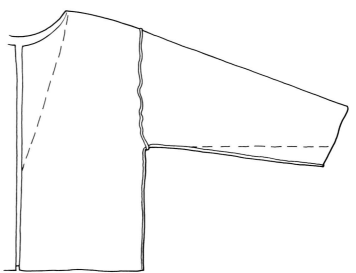

4. Measure the distance around all the raw edges (front opening, lower edge, sleeve edges, and neck edge. Add 24" to this measurement. This will be the length of bias strips needed for the binding.

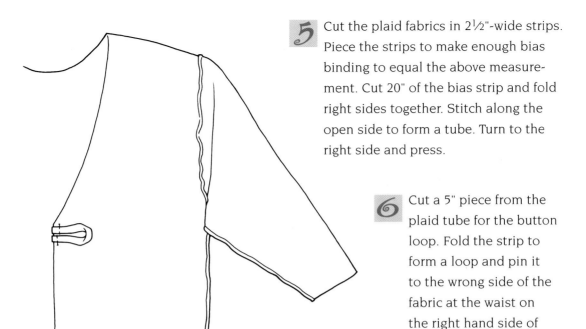

5 Cut the plaid fabrics in 2½"-wide strips. Piece the strips to make enough bias binding to equal the above measurement. Cut 20" of the bias strip and fold right sides together. Stitch along the open side to form a tube. Turn to the right side and press.

6 Cut a 5" piece from the plaid tube for the button loop. Fold the strip to form a loop and pin it to the wrong side of the fabric at the waist on the right hand side of the front.

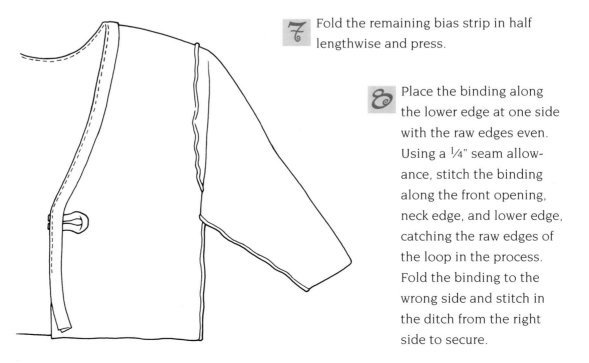

7 Fold the remaining bias strip in half lengthwise and press.

8 Place the binding along the lower edge at one side with the raw edges even. Using a ¼" seam allowance, stitch the binding along the front opening, neck edge, and lower edge, catching the raw edges of the loop in the process. Fold the binding to the wrong side and stitch in the ditch from the right side to secure.

9 Using the same technique as above, bind the lower edges of the sleeves.

10 Cut the bias tube into three pieces, 3", 5", and 7" each. Tie a knot in one end of each tube. Try on the jacket on and determine where the button will be placed. If the sweatshirt is oversized, the button can be placed off to the side for an asymmetrical look. Place the raw edges of the three tubes at the position of the button and stitch in place. Position the button over the raw edges of the tubes and stitch in place, through the tubes. Add shoulder pads to the inside of the jacket, if desired.

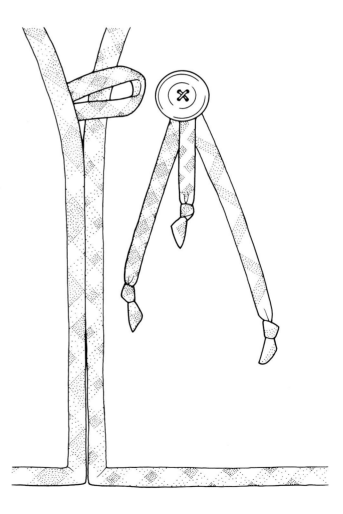

Cozy Denim Jacket

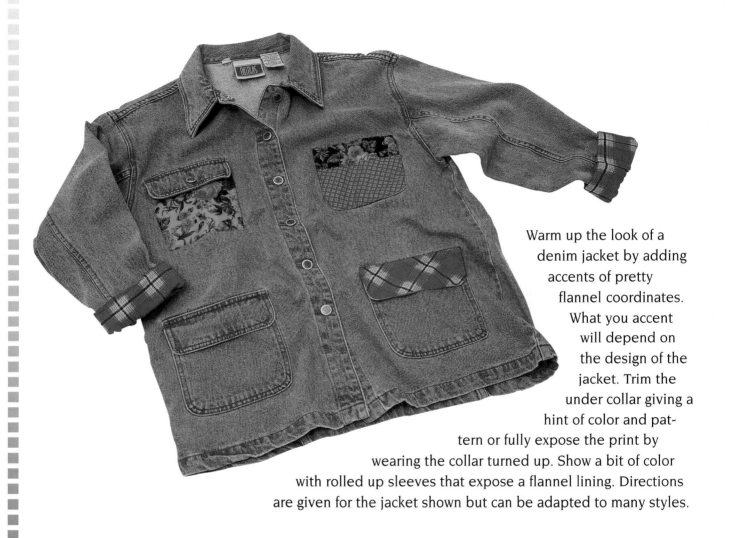

Warm up the look of a denim jacket by adding accents of pretty flannel coordinates. What you accent will depend on the design of the jacket. Trim the under collar giving a hint of color and pattern or fully expose the print by wearing the collar turned up. Show a bit of color with rolled up sleeves that expose a flannel lining. Directions are given for the jacket shown but can be adapted to many styles.

- Denim jacket of choice
- ⅛ yard of three to five assorted flannel prints
- All-purpose polyester thread (needle thread to coordinate with flannel prints; bobbin thread to coordinate with jacket)

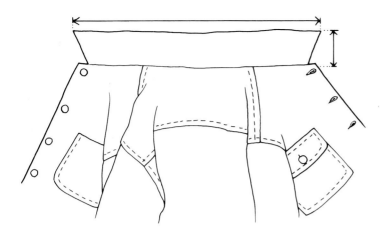

 Measure the collar at the widest and longest points and add 2" to each measurement. Cut a rectangle this size.

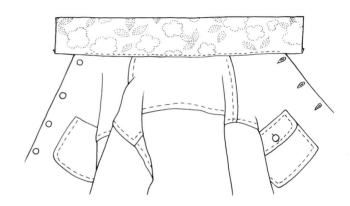

Press 1/4" under along the lower edge of the rectangle. Place the folded edge wrong side down along the lower edge of the under collar and edgestitch in place.

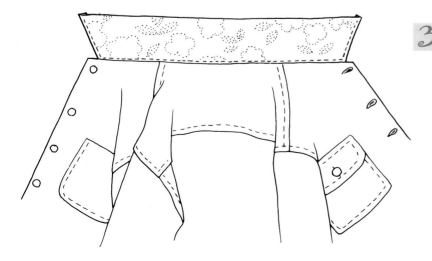

Smooth the flannel over the under collar and pin in place. Trim the flannel to match the shape of the collar, leaving 1/4"–3/8" extending along each edge. Fold the flannel to the wrong side along each edge, matching the edges to the edges of the collar. Edgestitch along the edges of the collar.

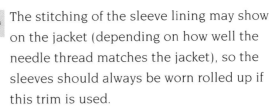 **4** The stitching of the sleeve lining may show on the jacket (depending on how well the needle thread matches the jacket), so the sleeves should always be worn rolled up if this trim is used.

Cut a rectangle of fabric 8" long and wide enough to go around the lower edge of the sleeve, plus ½" for seam allowances. If the sleeve is tapered, shape the rectangle to match the shape of the sleeve, remembering to add seam allowances.

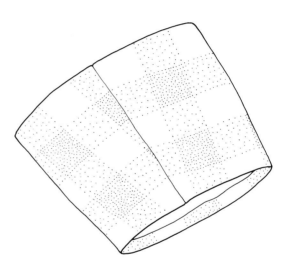

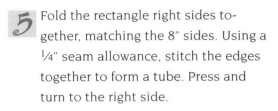 **5** Fold the rectangle right sides together, matching the 8" sides. Using a ¼" seam allowance, stitch the edges together to form a tube. Press and turn to the right side.

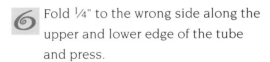 **6** Fold ¼" to the wrong side along the upper and lower edge of the tube and press.

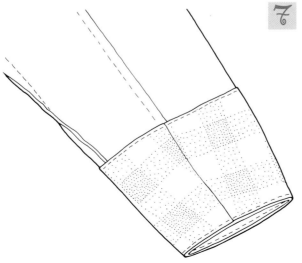

7 Turn the jacket sleeve wrong side out. Slip the tube up over the sleeve and match the lower edges. Using the freearm of the sewing machine, edgestitch the lower edge of the flannel to the lower edge of the sleeve. Edgestitch along the upper folded edge of the flannel to secure it to the jacket. Turn the sleeves to the right side and roll the edges up twice to expose the flannel lining. Repeat steps 4 through 7 for the remaining sleeve.

Pockets come in all shapes and sizes and can be trimmed in a variety of ways. They can be removed, covered, and stitched back in place; they can be removed and totally replaced; or they can be covered and trimmed while still on the jacket. The following directions show just one of the ways that pockets can be trimmed, so don't stop here! Come up with a few of your own.

Banded Patch Pocket

 Carefully remove the pocket from the jacket. Cut a rectangle of fabric 1" larger than the pocket on the sides and lower edges. Stitch a 2" strip of a coordinating fabric along the upper edge of the rectangle.

 Position the banded rectangle over the pocket with $\frac{1}{2}$" extending at the top edge. Trim the remaining edges to match the pocket leaving about $\frac{1}{2}$" extending beyond the pocket. Fold the top edge of the flannel to the wrong side and stitch in place.

3 Fold the edges of the flannel to the wrong side around the remaining edges of the pocket and press. Staystitch about $\frac{1}{8}$" away from the actual pocket. Fold to the wrong side along this stitching, clipping where necessary.

Tip: If the pocket has a rounded or curved edge, trace the pocket onto the wrong side of the flannel; stay-stitch $\frac{1}{8}$" from the mark.

 Position the pocket on the jacket and stitch in place.

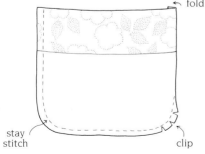

fold →

stay stitch

clip

Covered Pocket

If you have a free arm sewing machine, this technique works on a patch pocket without removing it from the jacket. Measure the pocket and cut one from flannel, adding $\frac{1}{4}$" around all edges. Fold the edges under and press so the flannel is the same size as the jacket pocket. Pin the flannel to the pocket matching edges.

Slip the pocket onto the free arm of the sewing machine and edgestitch the top edge, sewing through the flannel and the pocket only and getting as close to the side edges as possible. Remove the pocket from the sewing machine and edgestitch all other pocket edges, stitching through the flannel, pocket, and jacket.

"Bed" Jacket

Use a vintage chenille-type bedspread to make a fun, easy bomber jacket.

- ☙ Bomber jacket pattern with elastic casings at the wrists and lower edge
- ☙ Bedspread or pieces large enough to cut out jacket pattern
- ☙ Separating zipper for the front opening according to the pattern instructions
- ☙ Elastic and other notions according to the pattern
- ☙ Seams Great® (nylon tricot strips)
- ☙ Polyester or cotton thread for construction

 Cut out all jacket pieces following pattern instructions.

Tip: Before cutting out the jacket pattern, examine the bedspread for worn or stained spots and take them into consideration when laying out the pattern pieces. Determine if there is a pattern or direction to the design of the bedspread and, if possible, use it to enhance the cut of the jacket. For instance, the jacket shown was cut with the circular pattern meeting and matching at the center front opening.

 Assemble the jacket according to the pattern instructions using the following technique to enclose the raw edges and protect them from raveling.

Note: The jacket can be serged, however, due to the loosely woven nature of chenille bedspreads, the described seam finish will prove to be sturdier and more protective of the raw edges.

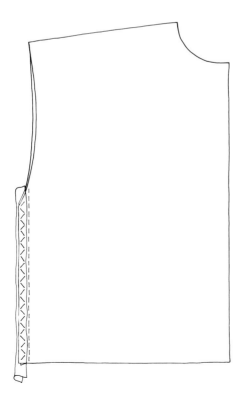

 After stitching the seam, place the Seams Great® tricot strip over the raw edge. By pulling on the strip, it will curl to the wrong side and easily wrap around the raw edge. Using a medium zigzag stitch, sew through all layers, securing the tricot and encasing the seam allowance.

   Finish each seam in this manner as it is sewn before stitching another seam across it. Press finished seams toward the back of the garment after the tricot has been stitched in place.

Fast Flannel Jacket

This lightweight, unlined jacket can be made very quickly using a man's flannel shirt. It's perfect for cool evenings when a regular jacket would be too warm.

- Large or extra large man's flannel shirt. The shirt needs to be roomy enough to wear over other clothing.
- ½ yard ribbing
- 24"–26" Separating zipper
- 5" x 8" Fusible interfacing
- Single-fold bias tape

1 Trim the lower edge of the shirt to about 4" below your waistline or hipline, as desired. Measure the new lower edge of the shirt and cut ribbing 7" x ⅔ of this measurement.

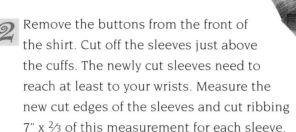

2 Remove the buttons from the front of the shirt. Cut off the sleeves just above the cuffs. The newly cut sleeves need to reach at least to your wrists. Measure the new cut edges of the sleeves and cut ribbing 7" x ⅔ of this measurement for each sleeve.

3 Cut two pieces 4" x 5" pieces from the excess fabric trimmed from the lower edge of the shirt. Fuse interfacing to the wrong side of these pieces.

4 With right sides together, stitch one piece to each short edge of the ribbing. With wrong sides together, fold the ribbing with the attached flannel pieces in half across the long measurement.

5 Measure the ribbing piece for the lower edge and divide it into quarters. Stitch it to the lower edge of the shirt, stretching to match the quarter marks with the center back and side seams of the shirt.

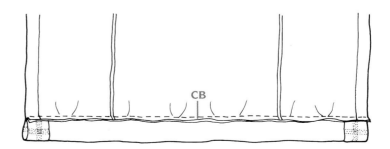

CB

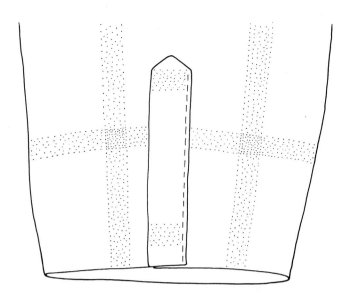

 Lap the placket of the sleeves and topstitch to close. Stitch the sleeve ribbing into circles and fold in half. Quarter and stretch to fit the lower edges of the sleeves.

Fold the front button and buttonhole bands to the wrong side and press. Place one side of the separating zipper behind each side and topstitch in place.

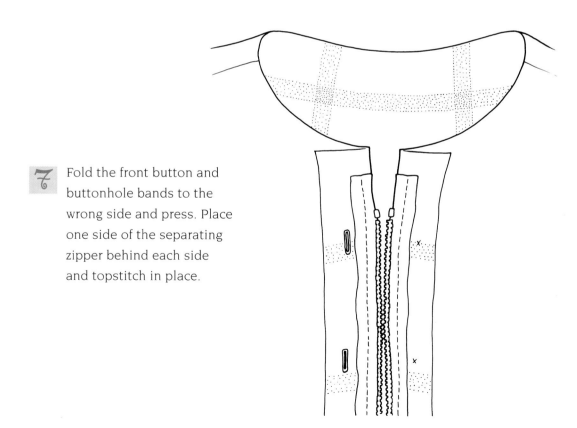

Remove the collar from the shirt by trimming around the neck edge. Cut a piece of ribbing 5" x ¾ of the neck opening measurement. Fold it in half and round the edges on one edge as shown. Stitch it to the neck edge, stretching it slightly to fit.

 Open one edge of the bias tape and place it right side down along the seam of the neckline. Stitch it to the seam allowance, stitching over the neckline seam. Fold the bias tape down over the seam allowance and topstitch in place, folding the ends under.

Optional Design Idea: Using the excess fabric trimmed from the lower edge, cut two pockets and fuse interfacing to the wrong side. Press under the edges and topstitch in place to the jacket fronts.

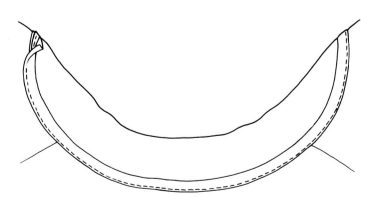

Chapter Five

Versatile Vests

The vest has a unique place in the line-up of fashion styles. More than a blouse, but less than a jacket, it completes an ensemble, accents a plain outfit, or offers a way to ward off a chill without the extra warmth of a jacket. Styles vary from short to long, fitted or loose, with darts, princess seaming, or one-piece fronts.

The design elements of the vests in this chapter include combining painting with embroidery, creating fabric from ribbon, and stitching together small pieces of fabric to come up with unique looks. Usually a quick garment to make, a vest can be made even faster by combining a unique front with the back of a ready-made man's vest.

Elegant Strip-Pieced Vest

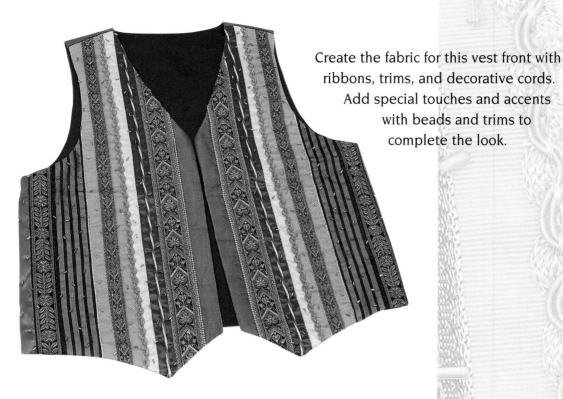

Create the fabric for this vest front with ribbons, trims, and decorative cords. Add special touches and accents with beads and trims to complete the look.

- Vest pattern with no darts or front seams
- 1 yard muslin—this will serve as a base fabric for the vest fronts. Any medium weight, firmly woven fabric will work, but using an off-white color will make it possible to use organdy or sheer ribbons as part of the front.
- 1 yard fusible interfacing
- Assorted ribbons of varying widths in coordinating colors (approximately 1½ yards each)
- Assorted flat trims of varying widths to coordinate with the ribbons (approximately 1½ yards)
- Assorted decorative cords and strands of beads
- 150–200 single bugle beads
- Fabric for the back of the vest
- Lining fabric according to the pattern
- Invisible thread for the needle
- Cotton thread for the bobbin
- Polyester thread for construction

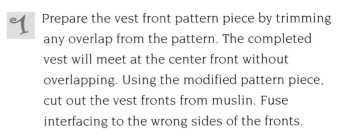

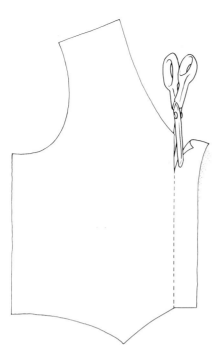

1 Prepare the vest front pattern piece by trimming any overlap from the pattern. The completed vest will meet at the center front without overlapping. Using the modified pattern piece, cut out the vest fronts from muslin. Fuse interfacing to the wrong sides of the fronts.

2 Vertically arrange the ribbons and flat trims as desired across the muslin vest fronts, placing them edge to edge. Once the ribbons are organized in a pleasing arrangement, pin them to the muslin.

3 Using invisible thread in the needle and cotton thread in the bobbin, stitch the ribbons and trims to the muslin. Set the machine for a narrow zigzag stitch and sew the edges of the ribbon by positioning the center of the foot where the ribbons come together. The zigzag stitch should be wide enough to stitch into both ribbons. Trim the edges of the ribbons to match the vest front edges.

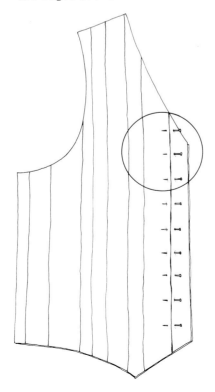

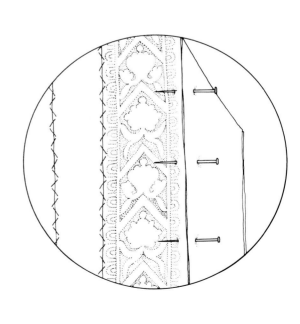

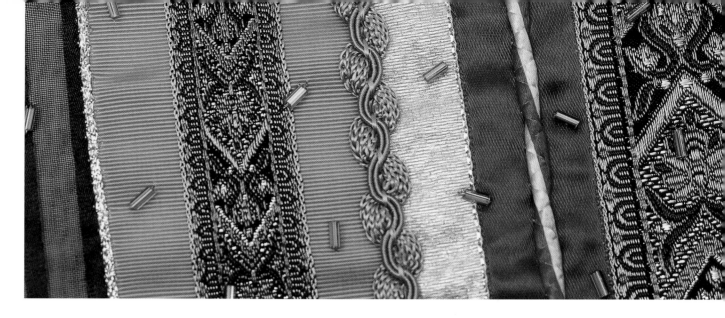

4 Once the ribbons are stitched onto the muslin, couch assorted strands of beads and decorative cords down the center of the ribbons and over the edges as desired.

5 Stitch the bugle beads over the fronts in a random pattern, avoiding the seam allowances. Complete the vest according to the pattern directions.

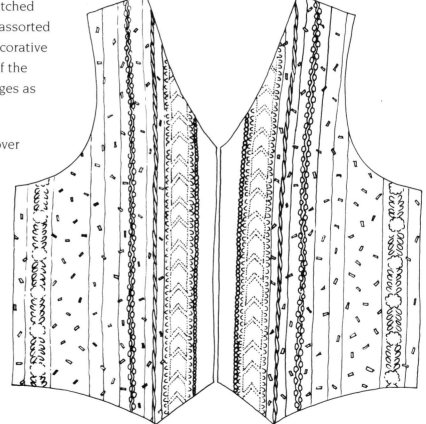

Fringed Pieces Vest

Make this unique fringed vest using
5" x 7" pieces of fabric and a coordinating trim.

- Vest pattern with one piece front
- 24–30 rectangles of linen, 5" x 7" each, for the vest front
- 1 yard of coordinating fabric for the vest back
- 5–6 yards of flat braided trim, ½" or wider
- 2 yards of 22"-wide fusible knit interfacing
- Lining fabric according to the pattern
- Fabric marker

1. Cut two rectangles of fusible interfacing, each one large enough for one of the vest fronts. Place each one *fusible side up*. Starting at the bottom-left corner of one rectangle of interfacing, place a vertical row of linen rectangles, overlapping them 1½". Carefully fuse them to the interfacing.

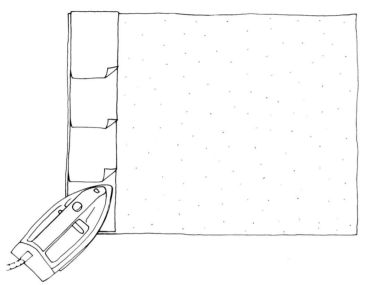

2. Place a second vertical row of linen pieces next to the first, staggering the overlap as shown.
Note: The first and last pieces will extend beyond the edges of the interfacing. Fuse this row to the interfacing. Continue placing linen pieces in this manner until the interfacing is covered. Cover the second piece of interfacing with linen pieces to match the first.

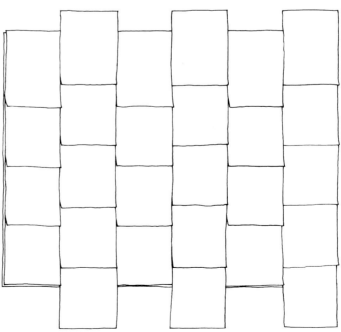

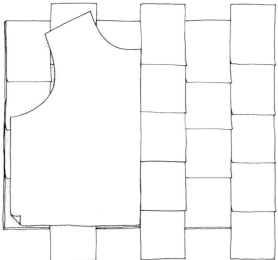

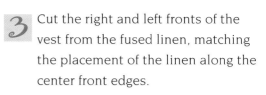
3 Cut the right and left fronts of the vest from the fused linen, matching the placement of the linen along the center front edges.

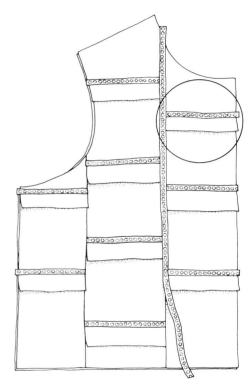

4 Measure 1¼" from the cut edges of the linen pieces. Using a fabric marker, draw a line across the linen at this point. Stitch the flat trim over the drawn lines. After all of the lines have been covered, position the trim over the raw edges of the vertical rows and stitch in place, covering the ends of the shorter pieces of trim.

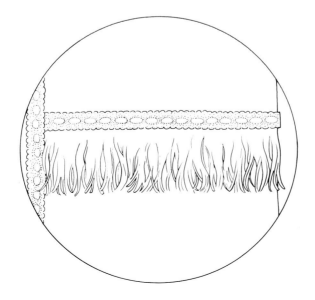

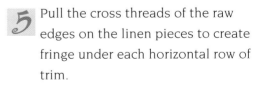
5 Pull the cross threads of the raw edges on the linen pieces to create fringe under each horizontal row of trim.

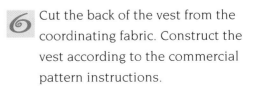
6 Cut the back of the vest from the coordinating fabric. Construct the vest according to the commercial pattern instructions.

Painted Embroidery Vest

Give new life to a plain vest by combining stenciling and hand embroidery to decorate the neckline. The subtle stripe of this silk noil fabric provides a distinctive background for the floral design. Outlining the painted design with pearl cotton gives definition and depth to the motif. It also helps to conceal the edges if the paint bleeds or smudges as it is applied.

- Vest made of fabric that is solid, striped, or has a subtle pattern
- Stencil with a floral or vine design
- Fabric paint in a strong contrasting color
- Small foam stencil brush
- Temporary spray adhesive
- 1–2 skeins of perle cotton in the same color as paint, or one shade darker
- Embroidery needle
- Assorted beads
- Buttons or button covers that complement the colors used in the embroidery
- Spring embroidery hoop

 Plan the design on the front of the vest, avoiding any buttons, buttonholes, or other elements that may interfere with the design. Spray the back of the stencil with adhesive and position as desired on the vest front.

Note: Follow the paint manufacturer's directions when preparing the garment for painting. Most suggest that the garment be washed at least once before the paint is applied.

Place a small amount of paint on a paper plate or wax paper. Load the stencil brush with paint and dab it onto the vest within the cut out portions of the stencil. Fill in the motif with paint. Reposition the stencil as needed to complete the design. Let the paint dry as directed by the manufacturer.

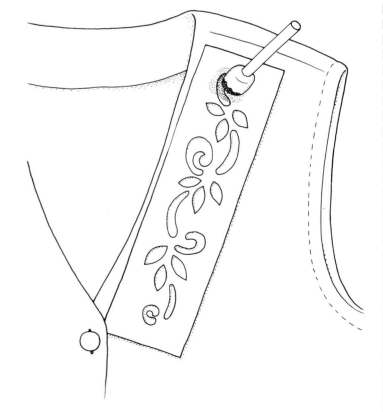

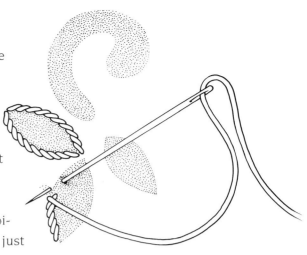

3 Embroider around the painted design with perle cotton using the stem stitch. Add any details desired within the painted areas.

Note: If you are planning to stitch within the painted areas, make a test swatch first. Depending on the paint, the surface may be soft or hard after it dries. Test to see if the needle will pass easily through the fabric areas that have been painted. If it will not, limit the embroidery portion of the design to stitching outlines, just outside the painted designs.

4 Add clusters of beads to the design. If desired, replace the existing buttons of the vest with decorative buttons that complement the vest fabric and the painted design.

Behind Bars Vest

Stitch up this striking vest front by piecing a bold print with narrow bars of a strong solid fabric. The solid bars break up the print to give it a more interesting look. For a speedy addition to your wardrobe, complete your creation using the back of a man's suit vest. The vest shown was made using a cotton drapery print and a plush upholstery fabric for the bars.

- 1 yard of a large, bold print fabric
- ¼ yard of fabric in a strong solid color found in the print
- ¾ yard medium weight fabric for the front lining
- Man's vest with a back that coordinates-with the vest fabric-colors
- Seam ripper

1 Cut eight strips of the print, 3" x 27" each (should be long enough for the vest front). Cut six strips of the solid, 1" x 27" (should be long enough for the vest front). Cut 3 to 3½ yards of 2½" bias strips from the print fabric (should be enough to go around the front armholes and the front opening edges of the vest). Cut two strips, 1½" x 18" each, for ties from the print fabric.

2 Using a seam ripper, carefully remove the stitches in the man's vest at the side and shoulder seams. The fronts of the vest will become the pattern for the new vest.

3 Using a ¼" seam allowance, stitch four print strips and three solid strips together lengthwise, alternating the print and the solid. Press the seams toward the print fabric. Repeat with the remaining strips.

4 Using the man's vest fronts as patterns, cut a left and a right front from the two pieces of pieced fabric. Do not add seam allowances to the man's vest fronts. Again, using the man's vest fronts as patterns, cut a right and left vest front from the lining fabric.

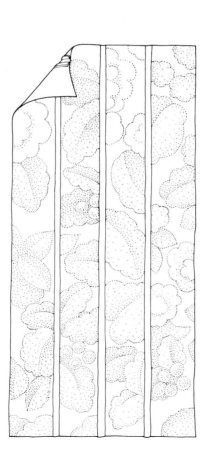

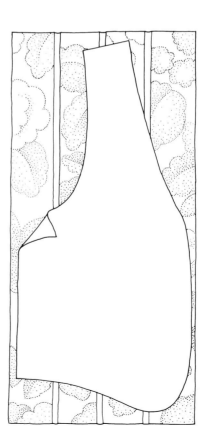

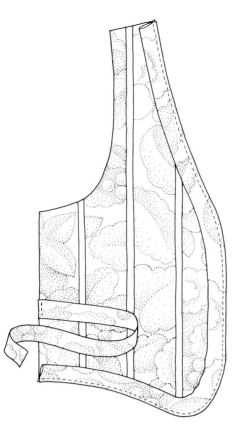

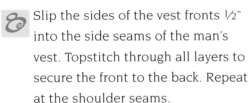

5 Place the vest fronts and lining pieces wrong sides together. Baste together ⅛" from all raw edges. Baste the ties to the side edges of the front at the waistline.

6 With wrong sides together, fold the bias strip in half lengthwise and press. From the right side of the fabric, stitch to the front opening edges using a ¼" seam allowance. Wrap the binding to the wrong side and stitch in place.

7 Bind the front armhole edges in the same manner, checking to see that the finished side edges and the finished shoulder edges are exactly the same as the vest back.

8 Slip the sides of the vest fronts ½" into the side seams of the man's vest. Topstitch through all layers to secure the front to the back. Repeat at the shoulder seams.

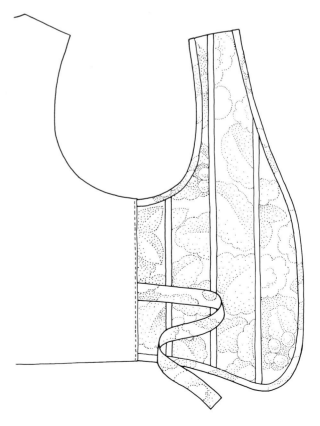

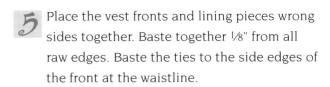

Denim Overvest

Less than a jacket and more than a vest, this comfortable top was made from a denim shirt to go with jeans, sweaters, and skirts. This shirt was one of several that hung in the closet rarely worn. Now that it's a vest, it's worn all the time.

- One oversized denim shirt
- Bias tape to match

1 Remove the sleeves of the shirt by cutting next to the stitching line. Enlarge the armseye by trimming about 2"–3" under the arm.

2 Using bias tape and a ¼" seam, face the armhole of the vest.

3 Trim the lower front edge of the shirt to resemble a vest front, continuing around to shorten the back. Serge or overcast the new lower edge. Hem the vest by turning up ¼" and topstitch along the edge.

Chapter Six

Delightful Dresses

The shirtdress has been a staple of American fashion since before the Victorian era. The bodice of the dress resembles a shirt, usually with a collar and cuffs, and a skirt is attached to form a dress.

The dresses in this chapter all begin with a shirt, blouse, or top. Fabric is gathered to the lower edge of the shirt and hemmed to the desired length. Even though the basic process is the same, the looks of the dresses vary widely because of the types of shirts used. Add a jacket, a vest front, or embellishments for a coordinated, pulled-together look.

Checkerboard Jumper

The checkerboard yoke and pockets of this gathered jumper are easy when you start with a bold, evenly striped fabric. Use this technique for yokes, cuffs anywhere you want to add interest and detail.

- Jumper pattern with one-piece front bodice and gathered skirt
- High contrast striped fabric with a stripe at least ½" wide—amount of fabric according to the pattern plus ½ yard. (The wider the stripe, the quicker it will be to piece the checkerboard fabric for the bodice and yoke.)
- Notions according to the pattern
- 1 yard of 22"-wide lightweight fusible interfacing
- 3–5 decorative buttons (optional)

1 Measure the width of the striped fabric and add ½". Cut several strips of this measurement across the width of the fabric.

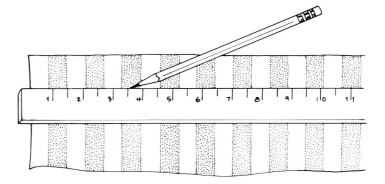

2 Using a ¼" seam allowance, piece the strips together, offsetting the stripes to form a checkerboard. Press the seam allowances down. Continue cutting and piecing strips until enough fabric is created to cut the front bodice and the pockets.

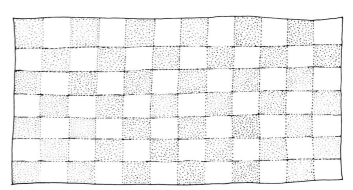

Right side

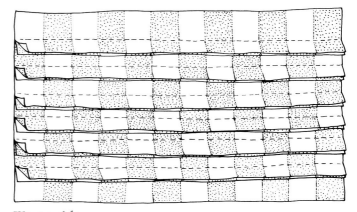

Wrong side

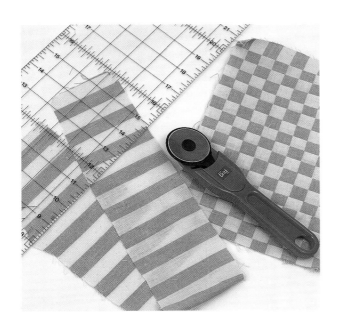

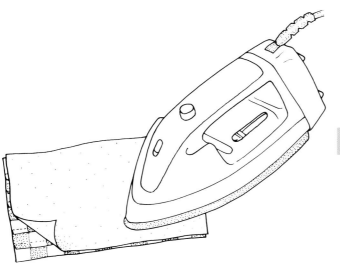

3 Fuse lightweight interfacing to the back of the pieced fabric.

4 Using the pattern pieces, cut the front bodice and the pockets from the pieced fabric.

5 Construct the jumper according to the pattern directions.

    Optional Design Idea: Sew decorative buttons down the center front of the bodice of the completed jumper. Insert a contrasting color of piping into the waistline seam.

Two-Piece Shirt and Skirt

This coordinated outfit started as a denim and corduroy shirt. The sleeves and collar of this long-tailed shirt were made of wide-wale forest green corduroy. Using the green color as the foundation of the outfit, two fabrics were chosen as accent pieces. The small check in forest green was used on the back yoke, pocket trim, and for the full, gathered

- Denim shirt—this can be accented with a second fabric as shown or can be made of denim only
- 2½ yards of coordinating fabric #1—this should be lightweight if you plan to crinkle the skirt
- ½ yard of coordinating fabric #2
- ¼ yard of coordinating fabric #3 (optional)—if the shirt is entirely of denim, a third fabric may be used to cover the collar and cuffs
- Fabric marking pen

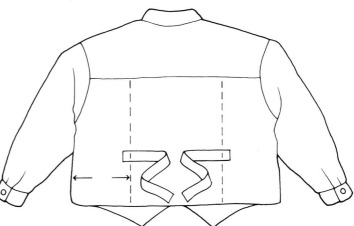

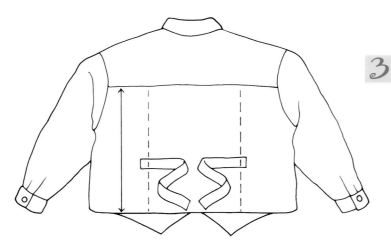

1 Shorten the shirt by cutting off the lower edge about 4"–5" below the waistline, shaping the center front with points.

2 Cut a 3" x 30" strip of fabric #2 for the ties. Fold in half lengthwise and stitch, using a ¼" seam allowance and leaving an opening along the center of one side for turning. Trim the corners, turn, and press. Cut into two equal pieces.

3 Using a fabric marker, draw two vertical lines from the back yoke down to the lower edge, 7" from the side seam. Place the ties at the waistline with the raw edge extending about ½" over the drawn line toward the side seam.

4 Measure the length of the back from the yoke to the lower edge and add 2". Cut two rectangles this length by 8" each.

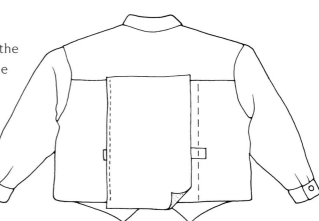

 With the right side down, place the raw edge of one rectangle on one of the drawn lines over the end of the tie. The upper edge should overlap the yoke about ¼". Stitch the fabric to the shirt using a ¼" seam allowance.

Flip the fabric to the right side and press. Edgestitch the fabric along the finished edge.

 Smooth the fabric and trim it to the shape of the shirt around the armseye and side seam, allowing about ½" extra. Fold the ½" under so the edges of the fabric lie on the seamlines of the shirt and stitch in place. Repeat with the remaining rectangle.

7 Measure the widest and longest part of the yoke and add 2" all around. Cut a rectangle of fabric #1 using this measurement. Place the rectangle right side down along the lower edge of the yoke, covering the raw edge of the previously stitched fabric. Using a ¼" seam allowance, stitch the yoke in place. Flip the fabric to the right side, covering the yoke, and press.

8 Smooth the fabric and trim it to the shape of the yoke along the neck, shoulder, and armseye, allowing about ½" extra. Fold the ½" under so the edges of the fabric lie on the seamlines of the yoke and stitch in place.

9 Measure and cut pockets according to the pockets on the shirt, using fabric #2, allowing ¼" extra around all edges.

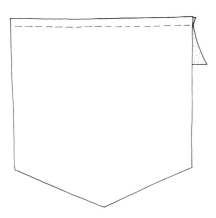

 10 Cut a band 1½" by the width of the upper edge of the pocket. Place the right side of the band together with the wrong side of the cut pocket piece along the upper edge and stitch using a ¼" seam allowance.

 11 Fold the band to the right side of the pocket and press. Fold the lower edge of the band under and edgestitch in place.

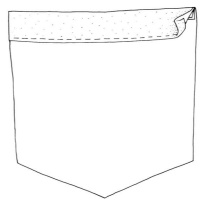

12 Fold under ¼" along the sides and lower edges of the pockets and press. Position over the existing pockets and pin in place. Edgestitch the fabric to the pocket along the sides and lower edges. Stitch the upper edge to the pocket only, taking care not to stitch through the shirt.

13 Turn the lower edge of the shirt up ¼" twice and press. Topstitch to hem.

14 For the skirt, cut two widths of fabric the desired length of the skirt plus 2"–3". Stitch the widths together to make a circle. Serge or overcast the upper raw edge to finish. Fold down 1½" and press. Edgestitch close to the folded edge.

15 Measure the elastic to fit your waist. Overlap the edges ½" forming a circle, stitch to secure. Slip the circle of elastic under the folded upper edge and snugly against the stitched edge. Using a zipper foot, stitch next to, but not into, the elastic to form the casing. Stop every few inches to slide the fabric back as it gathers around the elastic.

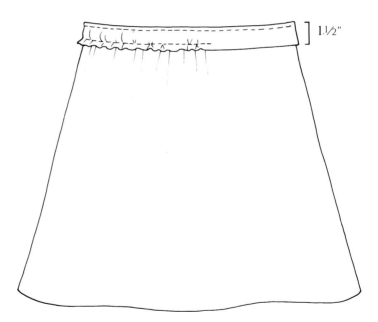

]1.½"

16 Serge or overcast the lower edge of the skirt. Turn up ½" to the wrong side and stitch in place to hem.

Optional Design Idea: To crinkle the skirt, wash and spin dry. Remove from the washer and twist lengthwise tightly. Slide a nylon stocking (one leg of panty hose) over the twisted skirt. Let the skirt dry for several days. The skirt may be placed in the dryer to speed up the drying process. Each time the skirt is washed, it should be dried this way to preserve the crinkled look.

Silk and Chiffon Dress

Create a shirtdress with a dressy feel to it by starting with a silk noil top and adding a chiffon skirt. Complete it with a vest front to pull the look together.

- Silk blouse or top
- 3 yards of a coordinating chiffon fabric
- 1 yard of fabric for vest front (linen, silk, rayon, etc.)
- 1 yard of lining fabric for the vest
- Yarn or decorative cord for the vest front
- Three or four buttons for the front of the vest
- Vest pattern

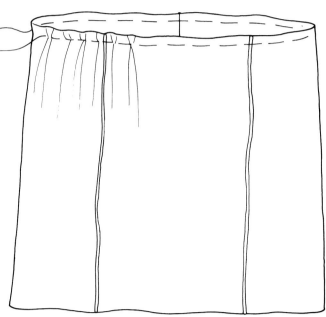

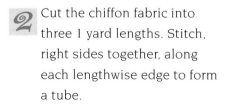 Cut the shirt to ½" below the waistline. Place a mark 5" from the center front on each side.

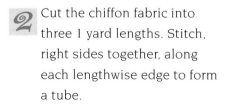 Cut the chiffon fabric into three 1 yard lengths. Stitch, right sides together, along each lengthwise edge to form a tube.

3 Using a long stitch, sew a long gathering stitch along the upper edge of the skirt about ⅜" from the raw edge.

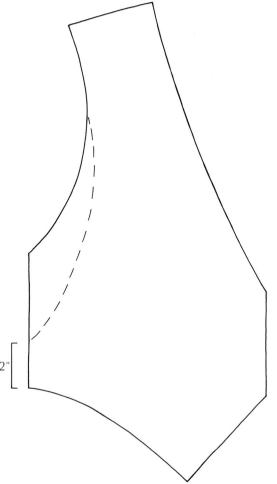

2"

4 Pull the gathering thread along the upper edge fitting the chiffon to the lower edge of the shirt. Match one seam of the skirt with the center back of the shirt. Match the remaining two seams with the marks on the front of the shirt.

5 With the right sides together, stitch the gathered skirt to the lower edge of the shirt using a ½" seam allowance.

6 Prepare the overvest pattern by tapering the armhole to 2" at the side of the vest. The shoulder seam of the vest should fit along the shoulder seam of the shirt. Adjust if necessary. Cut out the vest fronts and lining using the prepared pattern.

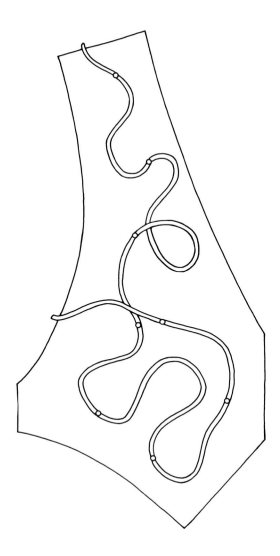

 Couch decorative cord in a random pattern on the vest fronts, avoiding the seam allowance area. Use a stabilizer or interfacing on the wrong side of the fabric if needed.

8 To make the ties for the vest, cut two 2" x 36" strips. Fold each one in half lengthwise, right sides together. Stitch along one end and the open side to form a tube using a ¼" seam allowance. Turn to the right side and press. Pin the ties to the side edges of the vest fronts with the raw edges even.

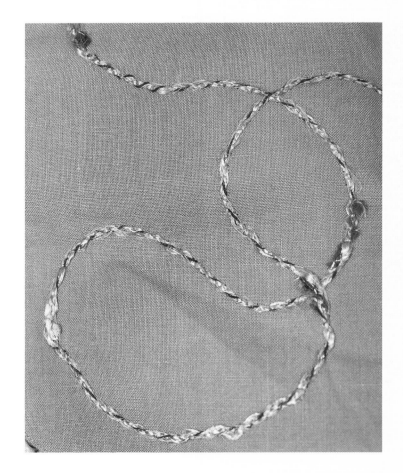

Place the vest fronts and lining right sides together and pin. Stitch along all edges except the shoulder seam, securing the ends of the ties in the process.

 Turn the vest fronts to the right side through the shoulder openings and press. Edgestitch along all edges of the vest fronts except the shoulders. Attach the vest fronts to the top at the shoulders by folding the raw edges under and edgestitching in place. Stitch a second row ¼" from the first. Add buttons and buttonholes to the vest front in appropriate spots.

11 Try on the dress and mark at the desired length. Hem at the marked length.

Plaid T-Shirt Dress and Jacket

Two purchased T-shirts and a plaid fabric combine to make this two-piece outfit. It's great for summer with its short sleeved jacket and sleeveless dress, casual enough to be comfortable and dressy enough to go almost anywhere.

- One short sleeved T-shirt with one or two pockets
- One sleeveless T-shirt
- 3 yards of plaid fabric that coordinates with both T-shirts
- ¼ yard of 22"-wide lightweight fusible interfacing

Dress:

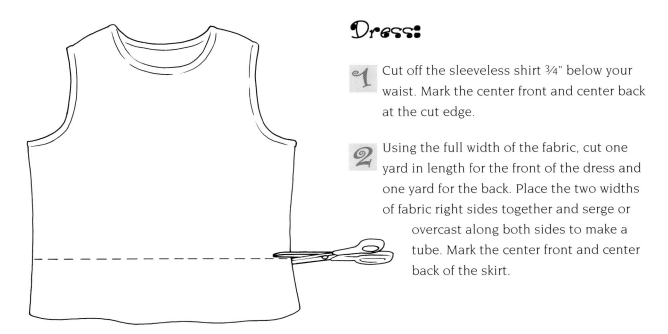

1. Cut off the sleeveless shirt ¾" below your waist. Mark the center front and center back at the cut edge.

2. Using the full width of the fabric, cut one yard in length for the front of the dress and one yard for the back. Place the two widths of fabric right sides together and serge or overcast along both sides to make a tube. Mark the center front and center back of the skirt.

3. Gather the upper edge of the skirt by zigzagging over a small cord about ½" from the raw edge. Use a medium zigzag stitch, wide enough to stitch over the cord without stitching into it.

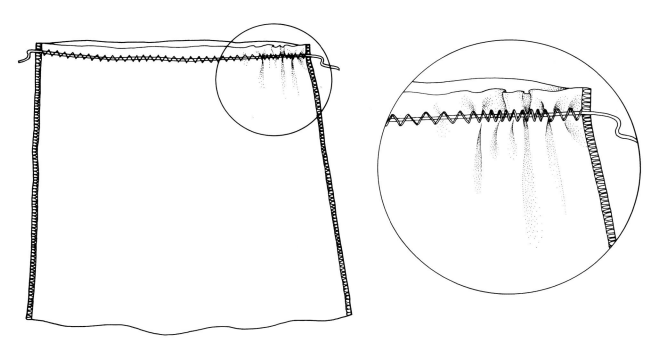

Note: Stitch one cord across the front, leaving 3"–4" at each end and stitch one cord across the back in the same way. It takes only a few seconds longer to do it this way, and it's much easier to pull the cord and gather the fabric over a shorter distance.

Pin the skirt to the T-shirt, adjusting the gathers evenly and matching the side seams and center marks on the front and back. Serge or overcast the waistline seam, using a ¾" seam allowance. The finished waistline should be at your waist or slightly above it. Press the seam up toward the T-shirt. From the right side, topstitch on the shirt about ¾" away from the seamline.

 Measure the skirt to the desired length. Serge or overcast the lower edge. Turn up ¼" and topstitch to finish hem.

Optional Design Idea: If the dress is too loose, make ties by cutting two 2½" x 12" strips. Fold each strip in half and stitch across one end and down the side using a ¼" seam allowance. Trim, turn, and press. Attach to the side seams at the waist by turning under ¼" and stitching to secure. Tie together as desired to give the dress a snugger fit.

Jacket:

 Cut off the T-shirt 5" below your waist. Find the center front and cut the front of the shirt along the center front line.

Note: To find the center front, fold the T-shirt in half lengthwise and press a crease down the center front. Cut along the crease.

Cut bias strips for the following: front opening—two strips, 3½" x 20" (1"–2" longer than the front of the jacket); lower edge—one strip, 3¼" x 50" (piece if necessary to get one long strip at least 1"–2" longer than the lower edge of the jacket); sleeves—two strips, 1¼" x 18"; pocket(s)—one strip, 1¼" x 5" (for each pocket).

3 Fuse interfacing to the wrong side of the front opening and lower edge strips. With wrong sides together, fold in half lengthwise and press.

4 For the front opening, fold the strips right sides together and stitch across one end of each strip using a ¼" seam allowance. Trim, turn, and press.

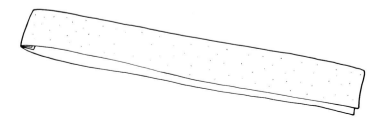

5 With wrong sides together, place the strips on the wrong side of the shirt along the front opening with all the raw edges even. Serge or overcast the bias strip to the shirt creating a band. Turn the bands to the right side of the shirt and press. Topstitch each band to the shirt along the folded edge of the strip and across the top. Trim the lower edges even with the shirt.

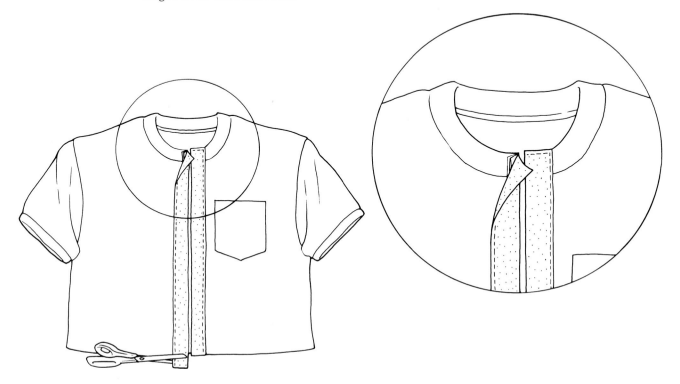

6 Fold in one end of the lower band ¼". Place the strips on the wrong side of the shirt along the lower edge with the raw edges even. Serge or overcast the band to the shirt. As you come to the end of the band, stop and trim it to ¼" longer than the lower edge of the shirt. Fold in the edges even with the lower edge of the shirt and continue to stitch. Turn the band to the right side of the shirt and press. Topstitch the band to the shirt along the folded edge of the strip and across the ends.

7 Measure the distance around the sleeve edge. Stitch a strip together to form a circle the same size. Repeat with the second bias strip. Fold the narrow strips in half and press. Place the band on the sleeve with the raw edge about ¾" from the sleeve edge and the fold closer to the shoulder. Stitch the band to the sleeve using a ¼" seam allowance. Fold the band down over the stitching and press. Edgestitch the band along the folded edge. Repeat with the second sleeve.

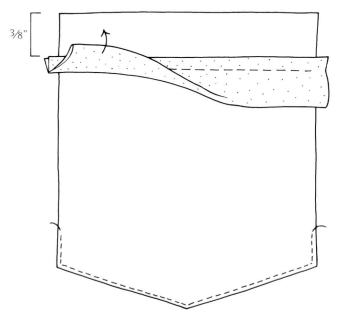

3/8"

 8 Remove about 3" of the stitching from the sides of the pocket. Apply the band to the pocket in the same manner as the sleeve; position it about 3/8" from the top of the pocket and wrap the ends around the sides of the pocket. Stitch the sides of the pocket to the shirt. Repeat for a second pocket if applicable.

Chapter Seven

Attractive Accessories

The key to a stylish look is the type of accessories used to coordinate the outfit. They can be anything from a scarf to a purse to shoes. Accessories set the tone for the look and help to make it elegant, casual, or campy.

The accessories in this chapter can be made from small pieces of fabric, discarded jeans, or remnants of another project. Most are quick to sew and can add the finishing touch to a great outfit.

Evening Pocket Shawl

A basic shawl is one of the easiest garments to make. Simply hem a long rectangle of fabric and you're ready to go. But with just a little creativity, you can turn it into an extra-special evening shawl. Add a ruffled collar and gathered pockets and it becomes pretty and practical at the same time.

- 2¼ yards of a soft drapable fabric (Finished shawl is approximately 65" long. If a longer or shorter shawl is desired, adjust the amount of fabric accordingly.)
- 1½ yards of 3½"-wide organdy ruffled trim with stand-up edges (This can be made from yardage by finishing one edge with a rolled hem over fishline and gathering the opposite edge.)
- 30" of rayon decorator cord (about ⅛"–¼" in diameter) for drawstring two small pieces of fusible interfacing, 2" x 1" each

1. Cut two 22" x 82" rectangles from the soft fabric. Set one piece aside for the lining. Fuse a small piece of interfacing on the wrong side parallel and 2" from the cut edge in the center of each end. Stitch a 1" buttonhole over the interfacing.

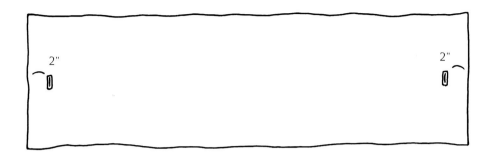

2. Fold the ruffled trim in half to find the center. Fold the rectangle in half matching the short ends and find the center. Match the centers and pin, right sides together, with the raw edges even. Pin the rest of the ruffled trim to the shawl, curving in the ends of the trim to the raw edge of the shawl. The trim will not extend the entire length of the rectangle.

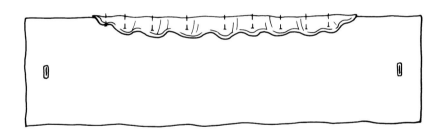

3. Place the ruffled rectangle and lining pieces, right sides together, and stitch along all sides, leaving an opening for turning at one end. After turning, edgestitch both ends, closing the opening in the process.

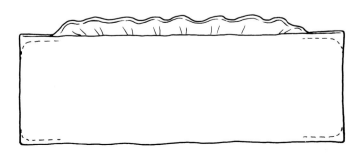

4 Make a ½" casing on each short end by stitching a straight line to the right and the left of the buttonholes.

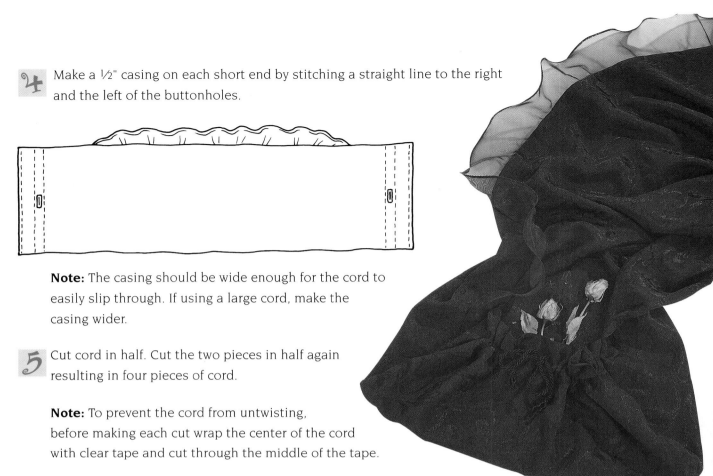

Note: The casing should be wide enough for the cord to easily slip through. If using a large cord, make the casing wider.

5 Cut cord in half. Cut the two pieces in half again resulting in four pieces of cord.

Note: To prevent the cord from untwisting, before making each cut wrap the center of the cord with clear tape and cut through the middle of the tape.

6 After cutting the cord into four pieces, add another small piece of clear tape to one end, extending slightly beyond the cord. Twist this tape into a point to give some stability to the cord for threading through the casing.

7 Thread the cut ends of the cords through the buttonholes of the pockets and feed them through the casing to each side. Stitch back and forth through the fabric over the cut ends of the cord to secure.

8 To form the pockets, fold each end up 8" to the wrong side. Stitch the pockets, gradually increasing the seam allowance and rounding the corner.

9 Turn the pockets right side out. Pull the cords to gather the upper pocket edges and tie into bows.

Zippered Tote

Once a denim skirt that zipped up the front, this large tote bag is quick to make and will hold all kinds of things. Great for taking supplies to sewing and quilting classes!

🌀 One denim skirt with large center-front zipper

1 Turn skirt horizontally on a table and refold so that zipper runs along the upper edge. The side seams of the skirt will now run across the front and back of the bag. Trim the upper and lower edges of the skirt 1" beyond the ends of the zipper.

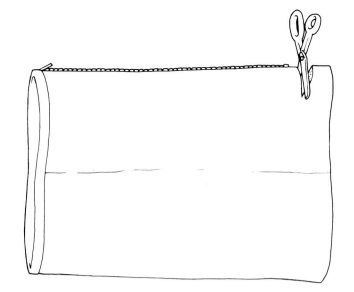

2 Turn the bag wrong side out and partially unzip the zipper. Stitch or serge the open ends using a ½" seam allowance. Turn to the right side through the zipper opening.

3 Using the excess fabric from the skirt, cut two straps 2" x 36" each. If necessary, piece the fabric to make strips this long(new fabric can also be used if needed). Fold under ¼" to the wrong side on each long side of the strap and press. Fold each strap in half wrong sides together and edgestitch the open edges.

4 Place the raw edge of one end of the strap about one quarter of the total width from the side of the bag. With the raw edge facing up, stitch it to the bag using a ¼" seam allowance. Fold the strap up over the raw edge and stitch it a second time. Repeat for the remaining ends of the straps.

To form the squared base for the bag, fold the corners into triangles, matching the side seam to the bottom seam. Measure down 1½" from the point of the triangle and stitch across the corner. Cut the triangle off if desired, leaving a ¼" seam allowance. Serge or zig zag across the raw edges to finish.

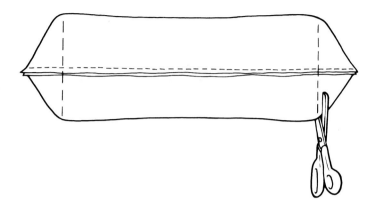

Optional Design Idea: Use decorative webbing on a contrasting fabric for the straps to add a design or color element to the denim bag.

Denim Mini-Bag

A cast-off pair of jeans and a piece of plaid fabric offer the perfect materials for this cute but sturdy mini-bag with strap. This shoulder bag will easily carry the basic necessities for a day's outing.

- One pair of denim jeans
- ½ yard of plaid fabric for lining and piping
- 26" of cable cord for piping
- ½ yard of decorative cord for drawstring
- 8" square of paper-backed fusible web
- 1" two-hole button in a color to coordinate with the lining fabric

1. Cut the legs off of the jeans at the crotch and open each one flat at the inseam. Remove one back pocket from the jeans. You can remove the stitches or cut the pocket out by trimming the denim from around the edges and then trimming the denim from behind the pocket.

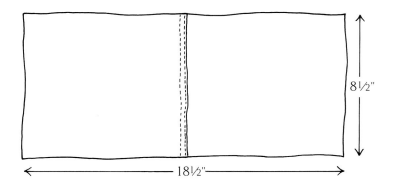

8½"

18½"

2. From one leg cut a 18½" x 8½" rectangle. Position the side seam of the jeans in the center of the rectangle. If the jeans are small, or of a narrow cut, the rectangle may need to be pieced. From the remaining leg, cut a 32" x 3" strip, piecing if necessary. Also cut one 8" square.

3. From the lining fabric cut a 18½" x 6½" rectangle, a 1½" x 26" bias strip, and two 8" squares.

4. At the center front of the bag (seamed rectangle), make a ½" buttonhole on each side of the seam, 1½" down from the upper raw edge. Cut each of the buttonholes open.

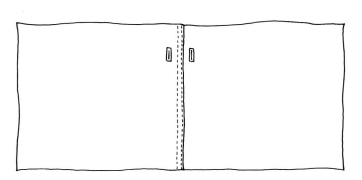

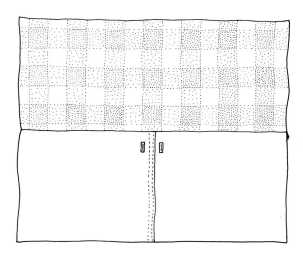

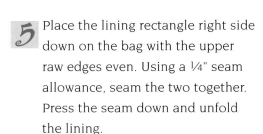

5 Place the lining rectangle right side down on the bag with the upper raw edges even. Using a ¼" seam allowance, seam the two together. Press the seam down and unfold the lining.

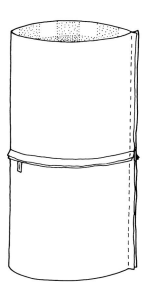

6 Fold the denim/lining piece lengthwise, with right sides together, and create a tube by stitching the long side using a ¼" seam allowance. Press.

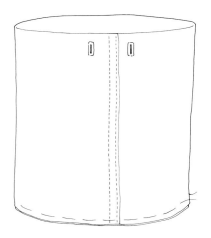

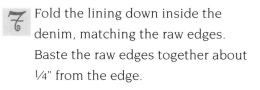

7 Fold the lining down inside the denim, matching the raw edges. Baste the raw edges together about ¼" from the edge.

8 Edgestitch the upper edge of the bag just above the buttonholes.

9 To form the casing, stitch a second row of stitching ¾" from the top edge of the bag just below the buttonholes.

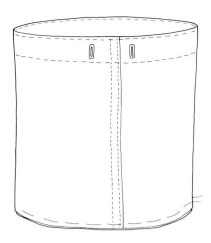

10 Following the manufacturer's directions, use the paper-backed fusible web to fuse the wrong sides of the 8" square of denim and one 8" square of lining together. Cut a base for the bag using the fused fabric and the pattern given in the back of the book.

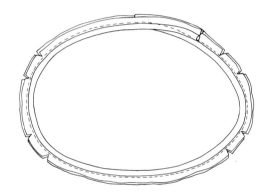

11 To make the piping, wrap the bias strip around the cable cording, wrong sides together, and stitch next to the cord using a zipper foot or a piping foot.

12 Stitch the piping along the edge of the denim side of the base, clipping the seam allowance as necessary to shape.

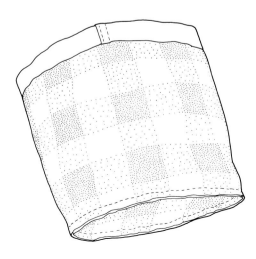

13 Turn the bag wrong side out. Place the base and the bag, right sides together, and stitch next to the cord to secure, using a ⅝" seam allowance. **Note:** The seam will be exposed inside the bottom of the bag and will need to be serged, overcast, or bound to finish the seam allowance.

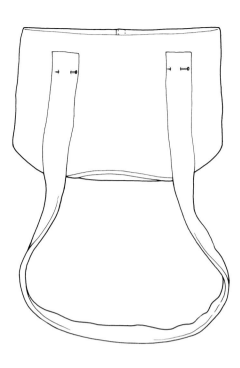

14 To make the strap, press ½" to the wrong side along both long sides of the denim strip. Fold in half, wrong side together, and press. Edgestitch along both long sides to finish.

15 Fold the bag in half along the upper edge, finding the center point of the back. **Note:** The original jean's seam is the center front. Pin the outer edge of each end of the strap 3" from the center back and 1¼" from the upper edge of the bag.

16 Using the pocket as a pattern, place on the remaining square of lining and cut adding an extra ¼" around all edges as seam allowance. Fold the edges of the lining to the wrong side ¼" and press.

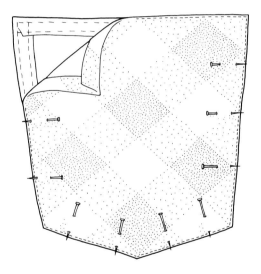

17 Place the pressed lining and the pocket, wrong sides together, and pin. Edgestitch along all edges to secure the lining to the pocket.

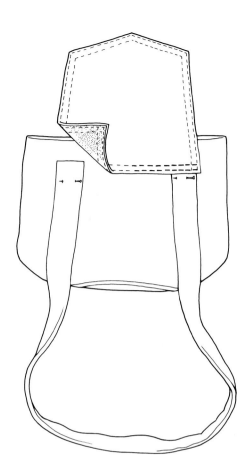

18 Position the upper edge of the pocket on the back of the bag 1½" from the upper edge and extending toward the front of the bag. **Note:** The pocket should cover the ends of the pinned strap. Adjust the position of the strap if necessary.

Stitch across the edge of the pocket to secure. Trim the ends of the strap to a scant ¼" from the stitching. Stitch across the pocket a second time ¼" from the first row of stitching.

19 Using a bodkin, thread the decorative cord though the casing with the ends coming out the buttonholes. Pull and tie to close the bag.

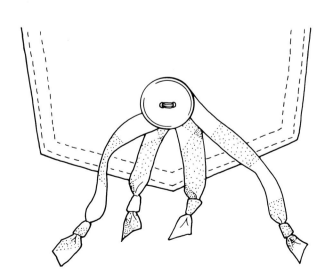

20 Cut two ⅜" x 8" strips of lining fabric. Tie a knot in the end of each strip and trim at an angle below the knots. Place one strip on top of the other and fold near the center. Place the fold on the front of the pocket flap as desired. Position the button on top of the strips and stitch in place, securing the strips to the flap.

Dressed-Up Sandals

Who would have thought the lowly flip-flop could be turned into lovely feminine sandals that coordinate with any outfit? They are so inexpensive and quick to make, you can have a pair for every summer outfit you own. Perfect for those backyard barbecues and Caribbean cruises!

- One pair of rubber thong sandals
- ⅛ yard of print fabric that matches or coordinates with desired outfit
- Glue gun with glue sticks
- Small silk flowers (optional)

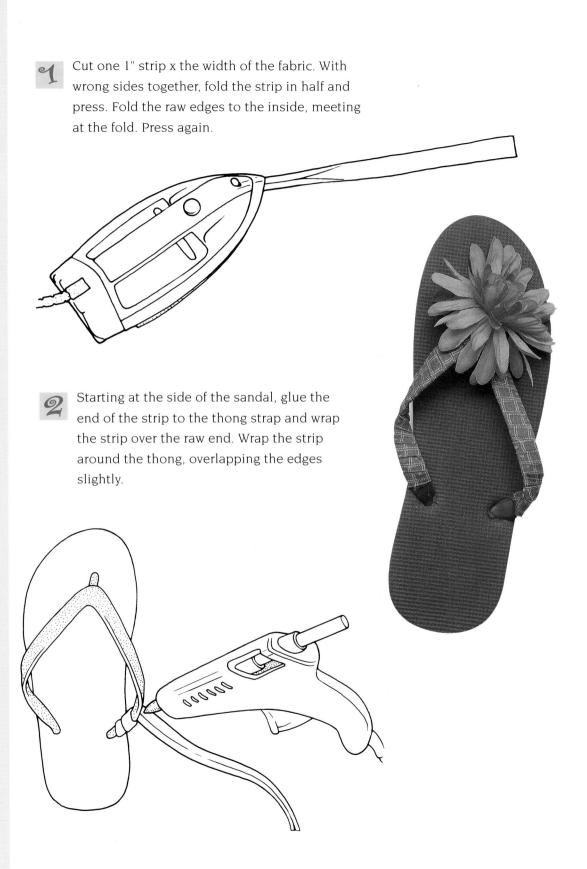

1. Cut one 1" strip x the width of the fabric. With wrong sides together, fold the strip in half and press. Fold the raw edges to the inside, meeting at the fold. Press again.

2. Starting at the side of the sandal, glue the end of the strip to the thong strap and wrap the strip over the raw end. Wrap the strip around the thong, overlapping the edges slightly.

3 Continue wrapping the strap up to the center and down the other side, trimming the end and gluing it to the strap.

4 To make a bow for the "toe" of the sandal, cut two 5" x 4" rectangles. With right sides together, stitch along all edges, leaving an opening in the center of one side for turning. Trim, turn, and press. Using a piece of the leftover strip, wrap around the center of the rectangle, pulling tightly to form the bow. Handstitch the center loop together. Handstitch or glue to the center area of the strap. If the fabric is limp and the bow does not lie as desired, handstitch the lower corners of the bow to the fabric wrapped strap on each side.

Note: The bow may be made smaller by cutting the rectangles 4" x 3".

Optional Design Idea: Glue silk flowers to the strap in place of the bow. For a denim pair, wrap the straps using a denim-colored cotton fabric (denim is too heavy). Create a frayed bow by placing a smaller rectangle of denim on top of a larger one and securing in the center with a denim strip. Clip in along the edges about ½". Wash and dry the bows to fray the edges. Trim to neaten if necessary and the complete the sandals following the directions above.

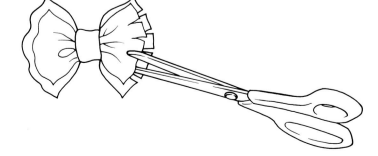

All-Weather Cowl/Hood

Make this self-lined hood from different fabrics for different uses. Use a soft silky fabric for a contemporary head scarf, a sweater fabric to protect against the cold, or a water-repellent fabric to keep your hair dry in a spring shower.

◎ 1 yard of desired fabric, 45"– 60"-wide

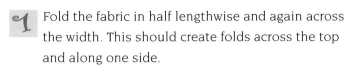
1 Fold the fabric in half lengthwise and again across the width. This should create folds across the top and along one side.

2 Place the pattern piece given in the back of the book on the folded fabric, positioning the marked edges along the folds.

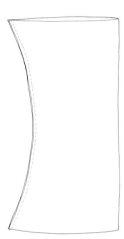

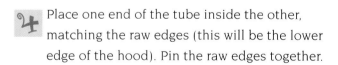
3 After cutting around the pattern piece, refold the fabric in half lengthwise with wrong sides together. Using a ¼" seam allowance, stitch or serge along the long open side, creating a tube. Turn the tube to the right side.

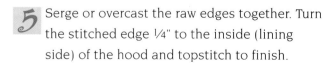
4 Place one end of the tube inside the other, matching the raw edges (this will be the lower edge of the hood). Pin the raw edges together.

5 Serge or overcast the raw edges together. Turn the stitched edge ¼" to the inside (lining side) of the hood and topstitch to finish.

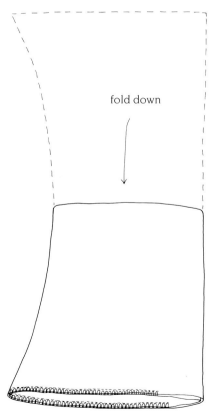

fold down

Fake Fur Neck Wrap

Keep the chill away and add an elegant accent to your winter coat or cape with this simple neck wrap made from luxurious fake fur.

- 1 yard of 45"-wide fake fur fabric—use a soft, fluid, velour-type fabric with a fake fur surface, many regular fake furs will be too thick for this project
- Hand sewing needle
- Strong thread

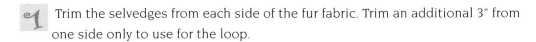

1 Trim the selvedges from each side of the fur fabric. Trim an additional 3" from one side only to use for the loop.

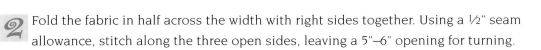

2 Fold the fabric in half across the width with right sides together. Using a ½" seam allowance, stitch along the three open sides, leaving a 5"–6" opening for turning.

3 Trim the corners and turn the fabric to the right side. Hand stitch to close the opening.

4 Cut a 3" x 10" strip for the loop. Fold in half lengthwise with wrong sides together. Using a ¼" seam allowance, stitch along the three open sides, leaving an opening for turning.

5 Trim the corners and turn the fabric to the right side. Hand stitch to close the opening. Overlap the edges about 1" and hand stitch the ends together to form a loop.

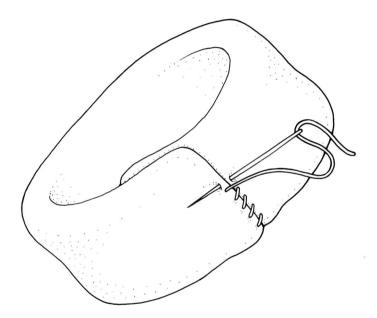

Note: After stitching the seams and turning the wrap to the right side, use a pin to loosen the "fur" from the seams, covering them up. Another option is to use a comb to pull the fibers from the seamline.

Accordion pleat the left side of the neck wrap and slip the loop onto it. Slide the loop up about 7"–8" from the lower edge and secure it to the back of the neck wrap with hand stitches. The loop will be slightly loose around the fur.

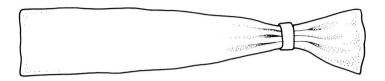

 To wear the neck wrap, place it around your neck, pleat the right end and slide it into the loop. Smooth and adjust the ends of the neck wrap as desired.

Note: If the chosen fur is too thick to sew and turn two layers, use one layer of fur and one of a color coordinated flannel for a lining. It will not be as bulky, but will still be warm next to the skin.

Origami Evening Bag

This unique drawstring bag is so quick
and easy to make, you can have one
for every outfit. Use a beautiful fabric
with rich metallic accents.

- ½ yard of firm fabric with body (may be interfaced)
- 4" x 4" square of plastic canvas
- 24" of ¼"-wide ribbon
- Four decorative buttons
- Hand sewing needle

1 Cut two 16" squares and two 4½" squares of fabric.

2 Place the large squares right sides together and stitch along all sides with a ¼" seam allowance, leaving a 4"–5" opening for turning. Trim the corners and turn to the right side. Press. Edgestitch along all four sides, closing the opening in the process.

3 Fold each corner back 2½". Sew the corners down by placing a button on each one and stitching it in place through all layers of fabric.

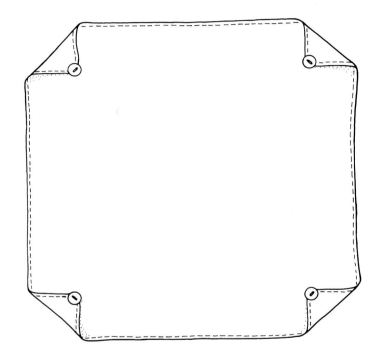

4 Make a casing by stitching ⅝" from each folded edge.

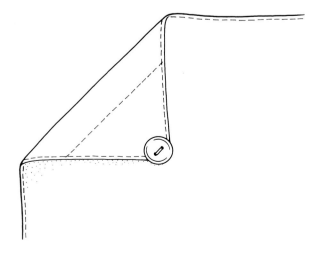

5 Make a 4½" dart on each side by folding each side down the center, matching the folded corners. Starting ⅝" from the folded edge on the inside of the bag, sew a dart to form the sides of the bag.

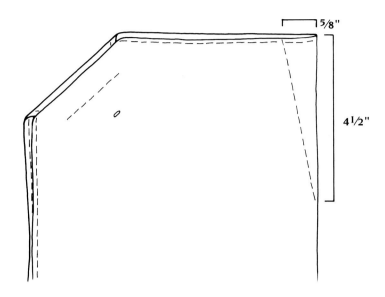

6 Place the two small squares of fabric, right sides together, and stitch along three sides using a ¼" seam allowance. Trim the corners and turn to the right side. Press.

7 Slip the plastic canvas into the pocket. Fold the seam allowances of the unstitched side to the inside and close the opening with hand stitches. Place the covered plastic canvas into the bottom of the bag to create the base.

8 Cut the ribbon into two equal pieces. Thread each piece through the casings and tie to form a circle. Pull each ribbon to close.

METRIC CONVERSION CHART

Yards	Inches	Meters
⅛	4.5	0.11
¼	9	0.23
⅜	13.5	0.34
½	18	0.46
⅝	22.5	0.57
¾	27	0.69
⅞	31.5	0.80
1	36	0.91
1⅛	40.5	1.03
1¼	45	1.14
1⅜	49.5	1.26
1½	54	1.37
1⅝	58.5	1.49
1¾	63	1.60
1⅞	67.5	1.71
2	72	1.83

METRIC EQUIVALENTS

INCHES TO MILLIMETERS AND CENTIMETERS
MM—millimeters   CM—centimeters

Inches	MM	CM	Inches	CM	Inches	CM
1/8	3	0.3	9	22.9	30	76.2
1/4	6	0.6	10	25.4	31	78.7
3/8	10	1.0	11	27.9	32	81.3
1/2	13	1.3	12	30.5	33	83.8
5/8	16	1.6	13	33.0	34	86.4
3/4	19	1.9	14	35.6	35	88.9
7/8	22	2.2	15	38.1	36	91.4
1	25	2.5	16	40.6	37	94.0
1 1/4	32	3.2	17	43.2	38	96.5
1 1/2	38	3.8	18	45.7	39	99.1
1 3/4	44	4.4	19	48.3	40	101.6
2	51	5.1	20	50.8	41	104.1
2 1/2	64	6.4	21	53.3	42	106.7
3	76	7.6	22	55.9	43	109.2
3 1/2	89	8.9	23	58.4	44	111.8
4	102	10.2	24	61.0	45	114.3
4 1/2	114	11.4	25	63.5	46	116.8
5	127	12.7	26	66.0	47	119.4
6	152	15.2	27	68.6	48	121.9
7	178	17.8	28	71.1	49	124.5
8	203	20.3	29	73.7	50	127.0

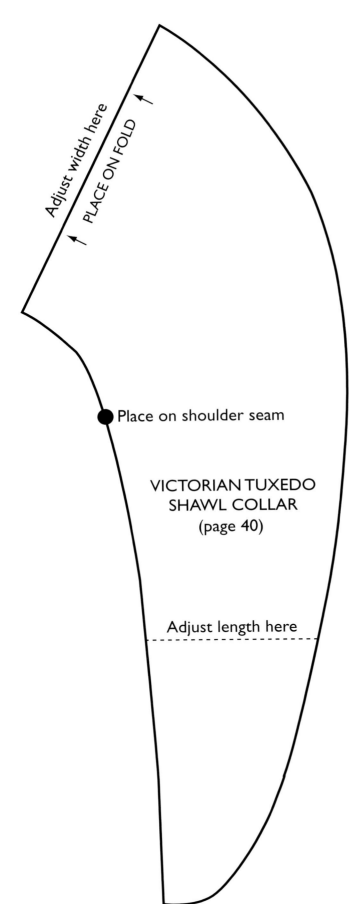

Enlarge 200%

Adjust width here

PLACE ON FOLD

● Place on shoulder seam

VICTORIAN TUXEDO
SHAWL COLLAR
(page 40)

Adjust length here

To check the fit, place the pattern piece over the shoulder of the tuxedo jacket, positioning the shoulder line on the shoulder seamline. The center back foldline should match center back of the jacket; add or subtract along center back, if necessary.

The lower edge should end just under the lapel above the button closure; add or subtract length as indicated on the pattern.

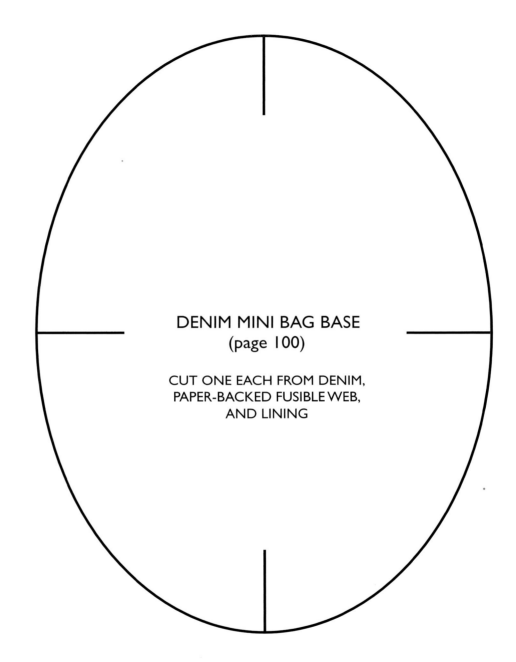

DENIM MINI BAG BASE
(page 100)

CUT ONE EACH FROM DENIM,
PAPER-BACKED FUSIBLE WEB,
AND LINING

Enlarge 290%

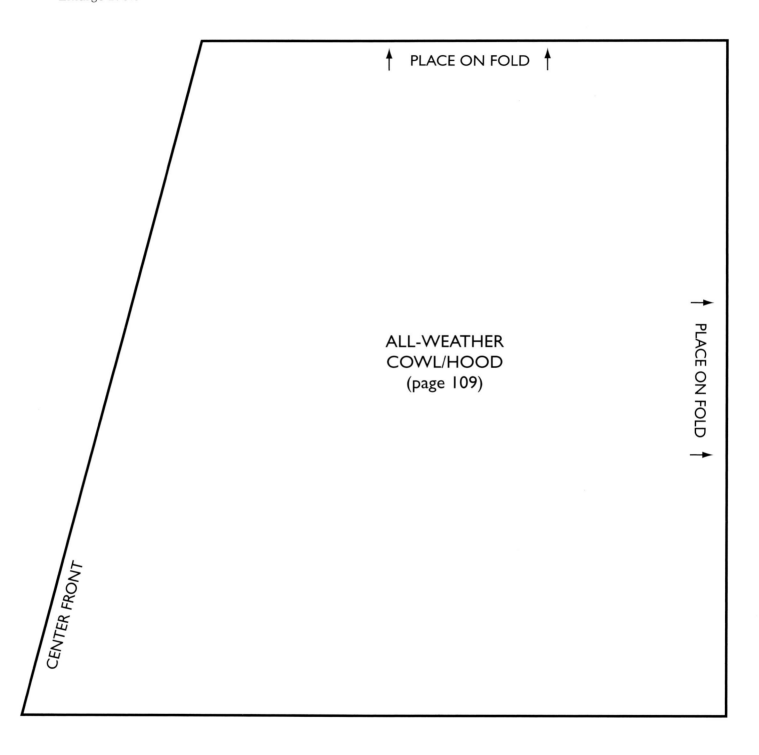

PLACE ON FOLD

ALL-WEATHER
COWL/HOOD
(page 109)

PLACE ON FOLD

CENTER FRONT

About the Author

SUSAN BECK has a degree in Textiles and Clothing and a Master's Degree in Design. Her long association with Bernina of America as a District Sales Manager, Educator, and Education Editor has kept her informed about the latest and the best machines, tools and techniques in the sewing industry. Susan is the author of *Quick Sewing Projects from Placemats* and *Second Stitches: Recycle as You Sew*, which was published in 1993. She has also co-authored two books, *Elegant Beading for Your Sewing Machine and Serger*, published by Sewing Information Resources/Sterling and *Fabric Crafts & Other Fun with kids*, published by Chilton.

Index

Index

Index

Index

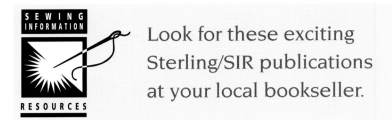

SEWING & SERGING TECHNIQUES FOR BLOUSES & SHIRTS by Laurie McWilliams

BEADING WITH SEWING MACHINE & SERGER by Susan Beck & Pat Jennings

QUICK SEWING PROJECTS FROM PLACEMATS by Susan Beck

DESIGNER TECHNIQUES: *Couture Tips For Home Sewing* by Kenneth King

SENSATIONAL SACHETS: *Sewing Scented Treasures* by Stephanie Valley

SEWING BEAUTIFUL PILLOWS by Linda Lee

SILK RIBBON MACHINE EMBROIDERY by Nancy Bednar

THE COMPLETE SERGER HANDBOOK by Chris James

APPLIQUÉ INNOVATIONS: *New Techniques For Beautiful Clothing* by Agnes Mercik

NoSew DECORATING: *Fast, Fun & Fusible Craft Projects* by Karen E. Kunkel

CREATIVE SEWING PROJECTS WITH YOUR EMBROIDERY MACHINES by Pamela Hastings

CLEVER CORNICES, VALANCES, & UNIQUE WINDOW TREATMENTS by Claire Martens

THE COMPLETE SEWING MACHINE HANDBOOK by Karen E. Kunkel

SEWING SHORTCUTS: *Tips, Tricks & Techniques* by Pamela J. Hastings

SERGER SHORTCUTS: *Tips Tricks & Techniques* by JoAnn Pugh-Gannon & Pamela J. Hastings